THE TRANSPARENT DETECTIVE

A SERIES OF SHORT STORIES

By

Arthur Allen

ISBN: 1-4107-7303-5 (e-book)
ISBN: 1-4107-7302-7 (Paperback)

This book is printed on acid free paper.

1stBooks – rev. 10/09/03

THE TRANSPARENT DETECTIVE

The modern city and rural life were too much for me when I returned from Vietnam. The attitude of the assholes I met and worked with didn't keep me from doing what I wanted to do in the way of getting money. I won the lottery and
after taxes, I had enough to get away from these people. I researched the land-grant thing the government had and bought 160 acres in the mountains. The property was near a lake, and I chose a spot on a small bench.

I passed through a small town and stopped to put a substantial amount of money in the local bank and met the local sheriff. He was a man of 6 ft. 6 in. and 265 lbs. with a big weapon on his hip. I introduced myself, "Hi sheriff I'M art miller and I'M going to live in the mountains about twenty miles from here, I want to build my own cabin or have it built. Do you know some one who can do that for me?" He smiled and said, "well IM glad to meet you and yes I do know a man who owns a construction company and can build almost anything."

He told me of this guy, but I refused and decided to build it myself, using modern equipment. I stopped at the local hardware store and bought, a chain saw, axe, couple of hand saws, hammer spikes, nails, etc. and then I purchased a 4 wheel drive vehicle and loaded the stuff on board along with a big tent for a temporary shelter. I began by digging a small cellar, about 12 x12 feet and as deep. The logs I cut were 14 feet long and I notched as most log cabins were. I split some logs to make the floor and made it a tight fit. All the logs fit nice and in 6 ½ months, I had it up. I called a company that built and installed solar panels and the things that went along with them and had them installed.

In the cellar, along with the solar equipment, I raised shelves for canned goods and jars of things I would can and store. Since I had solar power, I could use the electrical

equipment all households used. The kitchen had a fridge and a sink with a pump for water from a well that I found nearby. The water was clean and cold. In the wall between the kitchen and the living room was a fireplace that I used to cook with and to heat the place. The bedroom had a king-sized bed, as I like my space, a bureau and there were throw rugs in all the rooms.

On the outside was a porch that went all the way around the place and it was 6 feet off the ground. This was so I could stow an all-terrain vehicle and a snowmobile, along with

a trailer for the ATV and a sled for the snowmobile. I sold the truck and on the last trip to the town, I bought a rifle, a 30 caliber scoped rifle, and a shotgun with sufficient ammo for both weapons, as well as a hunting knife along with cold weather gear: clothes, boots, socks, and winter underwear.

CHAPTER 2

I built a small pier into the lake and to it I tied a canoe and a boat, mostly for fishing, but also for recreation. I got this all done before winter came and when it did, it was a dilly. Snow was over 6 feet deep in places and I had to dig out from the cabin to the lake. Then I got the snow mobile and the sled and started it and went to town. I bought a set of skis and snowshoes and binoculars. While there, I saw a set of puppies and bought them. They were rottweilers. I got dog food and some groceries. I got some mail, deposited some checks, saw the sheriff, got a short-wave radio, and left the call sign of aret k440 with him in case of emergencies, and drove the snowmobile back to the cabin. I put the puppies in a box until I could build them a pen.

I named them George and Chesty after the two generals I most admired, Patton and Puller, and installed the radio and tested it, "Sheriff, this is artk440, over."

He answered, "art k440, this the sheriff.'

" Sheriff, I'm testing the radio. How do you hear me?"

He came back, "Loud and clear."

I said, "I will be on the air at 12 noon and 12 midnight every day in case you or I have need for help from each other."

He agreed and we shut it down. A few days later, I was contacted by the government. They wanted me to take charge of the area in as much as the animals were concerned: to thin the herds and test the water and report to them. I agreed on the conditions that I got to keep the meat and hides of the animals I killed. The government man said "ok" and left by the choppers, the way he had came in.

It was winter and cold. I had bundled up and was on my snowmobile, headed for the mountain where a huge heard of elk was supposed to be grazing on a meadow. I got within a mile of the meadow and stopped the snowmobile. I went back to the sled I was towing and put on a pair of snowshoes and pickedup my rifle, a 270 magnum, and took off for the meadow. It took me an hour of steady moving to get to the edge of the meadow and the herd.

It was a big herd, but it had a lot of older bulls and I chose one and dropped him.

With a perfect shoulder shot, it dropped in place. I got two more before the herd scattered. I went back to the mobile and took it to the dead elk and loaded them on board and took off for the cabin. At the cabin I began to skin out the elk and cut the meat into pieces that were easy to handle.

About 50 meters from the cabin, I built a place to put the meat where animals couldn't get at it. It is a small house the size of a small tent and placed it on a cut-off tree that is about 12 feet off the ground. The house sits on a platform so animals can't climb onto it; the only access is a ladder. After putting the ladder against the platform, I put the meat inside. The cold would keep it fresh and frozen. Anything I had to keep cold, I kept there.

The hides I put away so I could begin to treat them in the making of clothes in the spring. I drove the snowmobile under the porch, shut it down, and pulled the sled in also. I went inside and after taking off the outer layer of clothes, I was making coffee when the radio came to life, "Kgq442 this is kcb212, " I answered with my call letters and heard, "Art, this is sheriff Mike Wood. I need your help. A small plane went down near you in the mountains. There was a man, a woman, and two kids on board and we need to find them."

I said, "Ok, I'll search the area and get back to you." I dressed in cold weather gear, took a rifle, and went to the snowmobile and hooked the sled to it and took off west. Earlier that day, I had heard a sound in that direction, like a landslide--a small roar. It was about half an hour later when I saw some color that didn't belong there

and steered in that direction. It was an airplane, a small one. I pulled up to it,

got off the snowmobile, and went to the plane. The wings were torn off, the tail broken like a giant hand snapped it off. I pulled open the door and saw a man, his face smashed against the dashboard. The woman passenger was also dead. I heard a sound from the rear and looked. There were two kids in the back; they were still strapped in.

I had to move the bodies to get to them and when I did, they pulled back. I said, "don't be afraid, I'm gonna help you get out of here," and pulled them out. I wrapped

them in blankets I bought along and then went to the bodies and went through their pockets for any ID. After pocketing it, I placed the kids on the snowmobile, wrapped the bodies in blankets and put them on the sled. I climbed on behind the kids and went back to the cabin.

I took the kids inside and they pulled back from the dogs. "they wont hurt you kids. They like kids." At the sound of my voice, the dogs nuzzled the kids. I went outside and moved the bodies into the cellar. The cold would preserve them until it began to thaw. I went back inside and the kids were asleep, lying with their heads on the dogs. I called the dogs off and took the kids in the bedroom. I took off their clothes and put them into something warm and into bed. I went to the radio and said, "kcb212 this is kgq442." Immediately, the call came back, "This is kcb212."

I said, "I got the kids and the parents are dead. I'll take care of them until you get
someone here to take them."

He replied, "Okay, I'll get someone there ASAP." I said, "Okay, Mike kgq442 out," and as I turned, I saw the boy.

He asked, "Mommy and Daddy are dead, aren't they?"

I moved to him put my hand on his small shoulder and answered,
"Yes, they are. I'm sorry. They died in the crash."

The little girl began to cry. The little boy took her in his arms and said, "It's okay sis. I'll take care of us." I put them to bed in my bed and I made a pallet in front of the fire.

CHAPTER 3

In the morning I was up and had breakfast on the stove. I had to go and wake them up. I told them "The shower is in there," pointing to the bathroom. Yes, this cabin had an indoor bathroom. The boy got up and reached for his clothes. "what

is your name?" I asked.

"John Wilks," he replied, "and that is my sister, Joan." his head nodding in her direction.

After a shower, I had them eat breakfast and went to the cellar so they could get their clothes, which I had gotten as they slept and bought them here. They went

to the suitcases and took what they wanted, that's when I heard the helicopter.

I put my hand on John's shoulder, "The sheriff is here to take you out." They moved to the door.

They took the kids and loaded the bodies of their parents on board and left. The sheriff stayed and would go on the next run. Over coffee he said, "They will be okay; their uncle is a rich man and he called me and will be waiting when the chopper gets there." We talked and made an appointment for a get together in the spring to go

fishing on the lake. He mentioned that he got a notice from the government that I was

doing okay in the thinning of the herds. "I got a couple of mountain sheep yesterday and they were big."

The chopper returned and the sheriff left. It was getting dark and another

blizzard was coming and it would be a big one. I went out and brought in a lot of

wood for my fireplace. The dogs were okay and fed, so I went to the cellar to get the hides ready to be made into clothes. I then took the hides to the big room and began to work on them, scraping the hide to get the leftover meat. There wasn't much; I would

have to wait until spring to finish the rest.

I started a fire in the fireplace and made a pot of coffee, adding a couple of handful of grounds in a full pot of water and eggshells to settle the grounds. I went to

11

the bookshelf and got a book and settled in for a hard winter. The dogs were playing on the floor, they were full-grown and still acted like puppies. The coffee was boiling and I got a cup and went back to the book.

I was drifting off and decided to go to bed. The dogs followed me to the bedroom; they slept at the foot of my bed on the floor. There was a potbellied stove in the room and it glowed red; I put a few pieces of wood in and banked the fire and then to bed.

I got up and went to the door, opened it, and was surprised when I saw snow. It covered the cabin; I was going to have to dig out, so I got a shovel and started. I went only as far as the end of the porch, as the snow sloped down to the ground.

I had made a tunnel and had to break my way to the meat stash, placing the ladder, which I dug out of the snow, against the tree. I climbed up and opened the door and got a side of bacon for my breakfast.

Back in the cabin, I got a couple of eggs and made biscuits and reheated the coffee. After breakfast I had to go on the

roof and clear the solar panels of snow.
When I had finished, I went back to the fire
and the book. The dogs
   were getting restless, so I let them out
and they romped in the snow. They were
chasing rabbits and I heard a snarl and
knew it would be a cat. I went in and got a
rifle, got into my snowshoes, and took off
after the dogs. I topped a small hill and
saw the dogs had a puma at bay. I called
them and fired as they cleared and hit the
cat
   in the chest, killing it. I packed it back to
the cabin to skin it and noticed that it was
the cat that had been killing cattle in the
valley below the mountain; it had
   a few bullet grazes.

CHAPTER 4

I had heard from old time mountain men that mountain lion is the best meat, so

I cut it up and stored it in my outdoor fridge. I took the hide in and put it with the others.

Spring came early. There was still snow on the mountaintops, but the lake was clear of ice so I put a line in and got some fish. The dogs, as usual, went in the water and scared the fish, so I had to chase them and it ended in play for us. I went into the cabin and began my inventory of food that I would have to get in town.

I had enough to last a couple of weeks and began to prepare the hides. I staked them out in the sun to dry and stretched them. When they were dry, I took them in the cabin and laid out one. Taking a shirt, I laid it on the hide and, taking a black marker, traced the outline of the shirt onto two skins, making the lines out from the skins so I could sew them together.

I needed to cut thin strips of hide so I would have something to sew with, but I didn't have enough. This meant I would have to get more by killing another deer or

elk. Besides, it was time for me to check the herd's sense that it was mating time. So

I got my rifle and took the dogs and my ATV/trailer and took off toward the herds.

I followed the herd for a while and found an old one that was lagging and bought him down with a well-placed shot.

I skinned it out and took the best parts of the meat and the hide. I could see

that nature's garbage cleaners or scavengers were gathering and I left the rest

of it for them. I returned to the cabin and took the meat to the outside fridge and took what little there was in it and transferred it to the one in the cabin. It was

full of fresh meat. I prepared the hide and cut the strips of hide for the stitches

for the shirts. I had some left over and cut pants from it. I punched holes along the sleeves, and sides of the shirts, turned them inside out, and sewed them together

as I did with the pants. I tried them on and they fit fine. I wore my belt over the

shirt that was left out over the pants; on
the belt was my knife, compass, and a
canteen for water.

A few weeks later, I decided to go to
town and got the ATV ready with the trailer
I made for it to carry things. I took my
rifle and one of the dogs, the other I left to
guard the cabin, George would watch it
and Chesty came with me, running
alongside
me as we left. We went over terrain that
was rough and there was no road until I
got near the bottom of the mountain and it
was a logging road that went into the
main road to town. I moved alongside
the road, my rifle was in the clamps
attached to the handlebars of the ATV. It
was about eight miles to town after I got
off the mountain and as I approached the
outskirts, I saw the people looking at me
kinda weird. Let them. I didn't care. I
pulled up in front of the store and said,
"Stay, Chesty," and the dog sat, he would
stay there and guard the vehicle till I told
him to move,
I went and began to gather the stuff I
needed, mostly canned stuff, coffee,

beans, corn. I saw canning jars. I asked the guy how to do the canning and his wife told me about it and how to do it. "I have never heard of a man canning

Food," she said. I told her, "Well, I have to do it," and thanked her and finished shopping. Besides the canned food and jars, I got ammo for the rifles and picked up

a whet stone to sharpen my knives, the one I carried and the ones I used in the

Cabin.

I left the store and put the stuff in the trailer and went to the sheriff's office.

He had a message for me; it was from a cop I knew in L.A. and he wanted to

discuss something with me. I asked the sheriff if I could use his phone that I would

pay for long distance calls. I got in touch with Mike and we talked about his bringing young people from The City to the mountains as part of a program he was trying

with kids. He wanted to bring them to the mountains for a week and try to help them get it together. I told him okay for later in the spring or summer and that I would call and let

him know what they were supposed to bring, then said, "No, I'll tell you now, bring jeans and long-sleeved shirts, changes of socks, underwear, and a hat, good hiking boots, and no,

I say, "No matches. None at all."

He said, " Okay, I'll let you know when we are coming."

"New clothes?" the sheriff asked.

I smiled and told him, "Made 'em from the hides I been saving and got fresh meat last winter." I asked about the kids that were in that plane crash. He said he hadn't heard. I left and went back to the ATV and Chesty

was holding off a couple of men who were looking at my gear. I asked them what was wrong. One of them lied, "That damn dog tried to bite me and I didn't do nuttin'."

I said, "That's a lie. Chesty doesn't do anything unless you touched my things." The store keeper came out and told them, " You're lucky that dog minds its master or

you would be chewed up now the next time you touch his stuff I'll let the dog
   bite you."
   I grinned and climbed on the vehicle, cranked it up and we left. Three hours later, I was coming up on my cabin when George came out to greet us. I went in and put
   everything away and went out toward the lake. I had built a small dock and there
   I had a rowboat and a canoe. I had to check them over to see if they were damaged
   They weren't, so I put them both in the water to let the boards in the bottom of the
   rowboat to swell and tighten up. I went back to the cabin, but on the way, one of
   the dogs ran up with a stick and I took it and tossed it into the water. Both dogs went in after it. Chesty got to it first, so I threw one at George and he happily
   went after it. Chesty came out and dropped his stick at my feet. I threw it back in
   and George dropped his and I threw it back in.

We played for about an hour, then I yelled, "Okay guys, let's get something to eat!"

They took off toward the cabin; I went to the closet where I keep twenty-pound bags of food for them and filled their bowls.

CHAPTER 5

It was the beginning of summer and Mike had called and we made arrangements for me to meet them at the logging road and I would take them the remaining twenty miles to my cabin. We, the dogs and I, were there the night before they got there.

It was sunup and I was drinking coffee when the dogs heads came up off the ground and I listened and finally heard them; they sounded like a troop of elephants.

I doused my fire, making sure it was completely out, and moved deeper into the woods. I kept track of them as they moved up the road; there were six of them, two each Black, Chicano, and White. I had told Mike to be sure they bought only the stuff I mentioned over the phone. I followed them for most of the morning and when they stopped for lunch, I stepped out of the woods. "Hi, Mike," I said. They stared at me. It was no wonder that they did, I was dressed in buckskins with a cowboy

21

type hat, long hair and a beard, my belt held bullets for my rifle and my big knife.

They stood up and one of the blacks laughed. I looked at him, "What you

laughing at?" and moved toward him as I drew my knife.

He backed up, "Nothin' man."

And his hands came up in a defensive manner. I stood staring at him and then turned toward Mike. As I did, he jumped at me and one of the dogs went after

him.

"Oh no! Help me!"

I grinned, "Back, George," I said and the dog backed off and sat

watching him. I turned to him, "I knew that's what you would do. You gang people are all alike. You and your friend there was also going to move. Him, I could have taken.

That's why I left you for the dog; you guys can't go one on one with a man or person who knows what they're doing so you gang up." I shook Mike's hand and told him

to have them take all the things out of their packs and lay it on their blankets.

One of the Mexicans asked why and I told him and them, "I don't trust you people,
so I'm going to see what you bought with you."
The black guy said, "What if we don't want to?"
I told them, "Well, I'll lead you into the mountains and leave you to the
bears and wild animals to eat. If you don't think I will, then you just try anything.
I will leave you hurt and alone."
They put their stuff on their blankets and I went through them. On one of the
Black guys' blanket, I found a pack of matches and took them.
"Hey! What you doin'?
How are we gonna start a fire?" he yelled.
"I'm gonna teach you how to do a fire without matches," I told him.
He laughed and said, "It can't be done."
I smiled
and said, "Well, you don't know everything there are two ways to do it and

if you'll shut your mouth, I'll show you in time." He didn't like that.

Most of them had bought only what they were told to bring, so I told them, "Pack it up and we will go to the area where we will be camping, so lets go." I

led the way through the woods. I was walking at my normal pace and they began to

complain right away. " Hey man, slow down!" one of the kids yelled. I turned and said, " If you can't keep up, then I'll leave you," and turned and kept going. I stopped about

a mile further and said, "Now you children can rest for twenty minutes," and I sat on

an old log. The dogs came to me and I scratched their heads. They then went into the trees

and soon a rabbit came dashing out with both dogs hot on his ass. The rabbit

was zigzagging. I laughed and yelled, "Come back here you two!" and the dogs slowed

and came back.

We started again and Mike was next to me when we started. "How much longer?" he asked.

" Oh, about three miles." The dogs took off toward the cabin. There

was still complaining among the kids and I just ignored it and kept on. In about

half an hour, we got to the cabin. "It's about time!" one of the kids yelled and took off toward the cabin. The dogs were on the porch and as the kid started to climb the stairs,

the dogs began to growl at him and he stopped and cried, "What the hell!"

I told them, "No one except Mike and me will go into my cabin." They began to bitch about it. "You will build shelters out here; that's what you are here for: to learn

some responsibility. You do that by doing what I tell you to do," I told them.

One of the black guys said, "Nobody tell me what to do. I'm leaving," and turned to go.

I said, "Okay, go, but how far do you think you'll get by yourself? There's snakes

and bears out there." That stopped him in his tracks. I said, "You have no idea where you are and how to get out of here. Now, if you'll come with me, I'll show you how to build them."

I moved to the trees and said, "There will be three shelters, two people to each and you will build them." I went to the trees and put my hand on a tree, "The crotch of this tree will be where you start." I handed one of them a hatchet and said,

"Cut some of those small trees about six feet long and as big as your wrist and bring a couple here." I took one and showed them how to lash the small tree to the branch told them, "Do this all the way across the cross tree and then lash some from the slanted pole to the ground to make the sides. When you've done that, cut some of those pine limbs and lay them over the roof and if you want to, you can weave the pine limbs in and out on the sides."

We watched as they built their shelters, I saw one of the blacks just standing,

"How about you? When you gonna start?"

He replied, "I don't do work."

I looked him in the eye and said, "You don't work, you don't eat, so get busy." He reluctantly went

to help his buddy. After they were finished, I checked their work and pointed out where they had made mistakes and helped them correct them. Then I said, "Okay,

I need a hole dug here about a foot deep." when one of them asked what for, I said,

"For your fire-pit. A couple of you start to collect rocks." When the pit was dug,

I told them to place the stones around the top of the pit; I took a small bag out of

my pocket, "This is tinder and you can make it by using a bird's nest or bark mashed up.

It is used to start a fire." From the other pocket, I took a piece of flint and pulling my

knife, I laid the tinder in the bottom of the pit, "Someone break small branches off that old log; real small ones and lay them in the bottom of the pit," I said then I struck the back of my knife on the flint creating a spark that landed in the tinder.

I blew into it and blew until a small flame appeared. I put it in the bottom of the pit and laid the small branches over it. "Get some larger sticks," I said and in a while had a fire going.

"That's cool," one of them replied.

"And that is one of the ways you start fire without matches," I told them. "I'll show you the other way later," I explained and stood. I then told them, "You can also use pine branches for a bed. Lay them on the ground and put your blanket over

them. That way, you stay dry; later I'll show you how to keep warm in winter."

Mike said, "That will be interesting."

I looked up and said, "You can also do this with smaller fires." I got a huge piece of bark from a tree and propped it up

close to the fire, "This is a reflector; it will throw the heat into your shelter if you make your own fire close to your shelter and put one up." It was getting near evening and I said, "Why don't you people go to bed or at least talk to each other. Anything that belongs to me is off limits to all of you. I may let you use things if you ask." I

Turned and went to the cabin and prepared my dinner and I sat on the porch drinking coffee and chatting with Mike; the kids were in their shelters.

Mike

said, "These kids are tired and I think they learned." As it got dark, he went into the cabin, as did I. I slept in my bed, Mike on the floor and the dogs on the porch

CHAPTER 6

I was up at sunrise and the smell of my breakfast cooking woke Mike and I told
him where he could find breakfast for the kids. Actually, I cooked it all: eggs, bacon, and biscuits. I went to the porch and yelled, "Come and get it before I throw
it out!" And the stampede began; it stopped at the porch. They had their plates in their hands and I served them and said, "This is your last meal I will serve you. From now on, you will have to find things to eat from nature." One of them asked, "How the hell do we do that?"

"That is one of the things I'm here to teach you: how to live off the land."
When they finished eating, they were told to pack up their stuff and get ready to move.

I got my gear and went to them and told them, "I'll show you an easy way to carry your stuff." I took a blanket from one of the kids, folded it in half, then took
his clothes and other items and laid them out in a row in the middle of the

blanket. I told the others to do what I did. After laying out the stuff, I then folded
the blanket so it was narrow, then folded it in half. I then took a piece of rope and
tied the ends together, forming a loop. I had the kid who owned the blanket
stand and I put it over his head, so it went across his chest from left to right.

"There, that is one way to carry your gear, of course, if you have a backpack,
then you don't need this." They all got their stuff together and we took off into
the mountains. We passed over a small hill and there was a fawn with her doe.

I stopped and pointed, "Look at that." There were a lot of cools and oohs and we all
stood still and watched for a while. We moved on; I was headed for a small valley I
knew that had a clean stream running through the middle of it.

We reached it at mid-day and at the edge of the woods, I said, "Okay, start building
Lean-tos and if you want, you can have individual fires, but be careful and don't
let the fires get away from you." I went to a place I had used before and laid

out my bedroll. The dogs began sniffing around for something to eat. I went to

watch them build their shelters and the one black guy that was a smart ass had

trouble because he hadn't watched when I told them how to do it. He went to

one of the white guys and said, "Build mine, or I'll kick your ass."

I went to him and

told him, "You won't be kicking anybody's ass. Get your stuff together and get out of here."

He looked around and asked, "Where will I go and how will I get out of here?" I told him, "I don't care how or where just get." As I turned my back he made his move at me. I spun around, raised my arm, and caught him at the ear. I threw an elbow into his face, breaking his nose and I went

knocking out some of his teeth. He fell to his knees and began to cry, "Please don't send me back by my self. I'm scared of the animals."

I helped him to his feet and took him to where his stuff was, and together we built his shelter and he shared it with the other black guy. I went to my small camp and began to dig a small hole for a fire when one of the kids asked, "When are you going to show us the other way to start a fire?"

I said, "Okay, I'll need two small sticks, one about 12 inches long, the other about two feet long, and two small pieces of wood." All the

things were bought and I cut the one stick at both ends, so one was rounded and so was the other. I reached into my pack and took out a piece of rawhide I had cut

from one of the animal hides and made a small bow. Laying them down, I took both of the small pieces and in one in the center, I cut a notch or a small hole, in the other

I cut another small hole and a notch at the edge. "Okay, this is called the bow method."

I took the 12-inch stick and twisted it so it was tangled in the bow. Putting the notched piece on the ground, I put some tinder under it, and sprinkled some sand on it to increase the friction. The other piece of wood I used as a holder; it was placed on the top of the 12 inch stick. I began to pull and push the bow and the small stick turned rapidly. In a few minutes, smoke appeared in the tinder. I dropped the bow and

blew on it. I got a flame and put it in the hole and added wood. "That is the other method of starting a fire."

They watched as I took two forked sticks and pushed them into the ground,

one on each side of the fire. Then I put one across the y. In the upright sticks

I took a branch and I cut it so I had a notch at each end.

I hung one end over the cross piece and my coffee pot from the other end.

I began to show them what was good to eat and what wasn't. I killed a snake

and skinned it and cooked it along with wild potatoes and onions. I made up a coating from flour I had bought with me and fried the snake. They all said it was good and I told them 'that is part of the survival' now. I went to the open area and

told them, "Now, I want you to get a big fire going and when you have it going good I'll be back."

They started by digging a hole and used both methods to start the fire, then they stacked wood on. I told them, "Okay, I want a long hole dug here about 6 inches down, and find rocks to put in close to the fire to get them hot." And I told one of them to bring

his blanket here. When the rocks were hot, I used the shovel to place them on the bottom of the hole and then covered them with a light layer of dirt. Then I laid the blanket on the dirt and told the kid to lie down on it and see if it was warm.

He lay down on it and said, "Wow, it is warm. I think I'll sleep here tonight."

I told him, "It will last three to four three hours."

CHAPTER 7

We stayed in the valley a week and while there, a bear and her cubs came down from the mountains to the stream. I told them, "All be quiet; she can't smell us, the wind is wrong. So, just sit still and be quiet." I passed a pair of binoculars around so they could see the bears. They stayed for about an hour and slowly left, trotting off to the north.

We left the valley and returned to my cabin area and the kids spent one more week in the mountains, and then they left. I led them to the logging road and said goodbye to all of them. The dogs and I started back when Mike stopped me,

"When I drop them off at the bus, why don't I come back here and we can fish and hunt?"

I said, "Okay. I'll make up another bed for you. I have another rifle and an extra pole."

He was back in a couple of hours and I had an extra pack made up. "I'm going out to check the herds and it will give you a chance to get a deer or elk."

"Great!" he exclaimed, excited as he took the pack and rifle I handed him. We headed north

and when we had come to the small valley, I saw the grizzly that was there before.

She stood and sniffed the air and came at us at a gallop. I went to my knee and began shooting. Mike stood and cut loose. The bear staggered and fell three feet

from us. I shakily stood and Mike was shaking. I prodded the bear; it was dead.

I took my skinning knife and skinned it out. I began the process of getting it ready for use as a rug and Mike watched, fascinated. When I was finished, I rolled the skin

up and we set off again north. We crossed the mountain and there were the herds.

We picked our way toward the herds. When we got close enough, I picked out a bull and said, "That one, Mike, hit him just behind the shoulder." He knelt and took aim and fired. The bull went down and the rest of the herd took off. I had bought my

ATV and trailer and we skinned the bull and cut choice pieces of meat.

We left some for the animals and as we left, they already were on the carcass. We loaded it all in the trailer and drove off to the next herd, where he got two deer.

We skinned both of them and loaded the meat and set out for the cabin.

As we came down off the mountain into the valley where my cabin was, a helicopter was landing. I pulled the ATV up to the cabin and went down to the chopper. The sheriff was there with the two kids I pulled from the plane wreck.

They also had their uncle there. "I want to thank you for saving my brother's kids and if there is ever anything I can do, please don't hesitate to ask."

I looked at Mike and motioned him over and said, "If you could donate to this man's cause, I would deeply appreciate it," and I left. Mike told him what he was doing with kids and the man offered to fund the cause for as long as Mike was at the head of it.

I watched as the chopper took off and Mike looked at me with moist eyes. "That was a real good thing you did, my friend."

"No sweat, my friend," I said and we unloaded the trailer, putting them in the freezer and the hides out in the sun.

We settled into the cabin, had supper, and sat on the porch sipping coffee and talked. In the morning, we took the canoe and loaded the fishing gear. We paddled toward a small island and cast the lines in the overhanging bushes at the shore.

In a few minutes, Mike had a bite and hooked a trout. "Well do you want to eat it or let it go?" He looked at it and said, "I'll let it go," and he took the hook out of the fish's mouth and set it back in the lake. I caught four medium trout and told Mike "supper" and put them in my basket and we paddled back to the dock.

I took the fish inside, cleaned them, and put them in the pan on the fireplace.

Then I cut up some spuds and corn and cooked them with the fish. We ate on the porch, finished and went to bed. In the morning, I taught Mike how to finished curing the hides and I finished the bearskin and put it in front of the fireplace.

In three weeks, Mike left and I returned to the cabin and to the life I came to love and with my two best friends, Chesty and George. I sat on the porch and

smoked my cigars and looked into the sunset.

THE END

SURVIVAL

Arthur Allen

CHAPTER ONE

He opened his eyes to darkness, raised his hand to his head, and felt the dampness; blood, he thought, and tried to move, but couldn't. A strap was holding him; he rubbed his eyes and light appeared. He looked around and found he was in a plane.

He then remembered that he was on a small plane that carried six people; he looked around and found the others. He felt around and found the release to the seat belt and moved it. he fell on his head and it hurt. He went to the others and found them dead. He was the only one alive and he didn't know why he was spared.

He kicked the door open and looked out. He was in a heavily wooded area and he got out of the plane and held onto the plane as his head cleared he moved to the baggage compartment to get his bags out. When he did, he looked through it and found a towel. He rubbed it over his head and it came away bloody; he rummaged through the bag and found a mirror. He looked and saw that he had a small cut where his head hit the rear of the front seat. He went to the plane and moved the bodies of the dead and got the first aid kit. Taking the mirror, he cleaned the wound and bandaged it then he went to the dead and going through their pockets, he gathered all their possessions. He would save them for the next of kin.

Looking about the plane, he was looking for something to dig with; he found a shovel, a military one, it was small but it would have to do. It was in the cargo area. He went into the woods and found a place where the ground was soft and began to dig. He dug three holes each, about five feet deep and carried the bodies to the holes. Wrapping each in a blanket, he placed them in the graves and filled them in. He marked each and said a prayer.

He returned to the plane to get stuff that would help him survive this ordeal.

He started by looking in the cabin. The compass was screwed to the panel and he ripped it off; it still worked. He went to the cargo compartment and began to go through the baggage. In his, he went after the hunting knife he had there and he threaded his belt through the loop on it. The bag had shoulder straps, so he decided to use it like a pack and took only the things he could use. He went through the rest of the luggage and found a winter parka, which he packed in

the bag. He packed five pairs of pants and a lot of socks; he found a pair of boots that fit him and put them in the bag.

He found three canteens and used one to carry fuel, which he got by stabbing the knife into the wing to get to a fuel tank and filled it almost full. He cut the

seat belts out and packed them, they could come in handy. Looking further, he found a couple more blankets, which he put in the bag. He closed the bag and, using the compass, took off south, which was the direction they were coming from.

CHAPTER TWO

He remembered that the plane had been in the air for about four hours. That meant they had gone quite a ways. One of the things he had taken the cockpit was a map; it covered quite an area. Using the compass from the plane and the map, he located the plane and marked it on the map for the purpose of locating it later.

Using the compass, he shot an azimuth in the direction he wanted to go and started off. He had gone only a short distance when he decided to cut a walking stick; he located a small sapling that was the size of his wrist and cut it down.

He trimmed the branches and had a fork at one end. At this time, he decided to change into a pair of his old combat boots; they would help him in walking a long distance.

He shouldered the bag and proceeded on his way. As he passed a rock formation, he saw a snake and killed it. Further along, he found wild onions and put them in his pack and also some herbs he found. He had rounded a corner and he saw a cave and slowly approached it. He took the flashlight he had taken from the plane and

turned it on as he entered the cave. The cave was about seven feet high and it went back about ten feet. As he slowly panned the light, he hoped a bear wasn't here.

There was no indication of occupation by animals, so he dropped the bag and began to unpack it. He had taken some clothes from the others to help in keeping him warm in case it snowed and got cold. After he piled the clothes, he went out and cut wood. He had to hack at some trees, old ones that wouldn't smoke too badly. He also picked up a lot of dead stuff off the ground; he stacked it

in a corner. He then began the process of starting a fire. Since he didn't have any matches, he had to go with old fashion methods. Taking a length of rawhide from his pocket and putting it aside, he went outside and cut a stick about the length of his forearm, then he cut two notches in the ends and then he cut the ends off a piece of fire wood. Using the tip of the knife, he dug a small hole in the ends of two of these, and he then cut another piece of wood as long as his foot. Tying the rawhide to the longer stick, he made a bow and then he set that aside and went looking

for some tinder.

He found it in a bird's nest that was abandoned. He pulled it apart and rolled it

in a circular motion between his palms. Placing it on the ground, he placed wood

in a small tower, starting with small pieces. Taking the bow, he twisted the other stick into the rawhide and then placing one end in one of the pieces of wood, he put the other end in the other piece of wood. Taking it in his left hand and the bow in his right, he began a sawing motion, going faster and faster until smoke began to appear, then a small flame.

He took the tinder up and slowly and gently began to blow on it, bringing the flame up, then set it in the tower and it caught the smaller sticks. He added larger ones to the fire until he had a good fire going.

CHAPTER THREE

After he had the fire going he went through the clothing and sorted it out so he would have easy access to the items. He would need food and a way to get it. He would have to make a bow, but needed certain things that he didn't have.

He would have to set some traps. Hoping he might trap a deer, he went out and looked for the material for which to do it.

While looking, he saw a rabbit hole and using a forked stick, he inserted the forked end into the hole and felt the animal move. He twisted the stick and pulled it out along with the rabbit. He chopped it behind the head, breaking its neck. He carried it to a fallen log that was lying near a path and laid the carcass nearby and took some rawhide from his pocket and looked for a way to raise the log.

Making a loop, he looped it around the log, stringing it up and through a notch made by a branch. He pulled it until the log was in the air, then placing a forked stick under it, he ran the rawhide around it and tied it off for the time being. Taking the rabbit, he tied it with the other end of the rawhide and laid it in the path. A deer coming to the rabbit would pull it and cause the log to fall, thus breaking its back.

He returned to the cave and carefully put out the fire and relocated it. The cave was shaped like the letter "L"; when entering it, took a turn to the right and he placed the fire out of the wind around the corner. After restarting it, he laid his bed on the ground next to it and set up the cave to live in. He had seen a stream while looking for a trap site, so he picked up the water bottles he took from the plane and went to fill them and returned to the cave to sleep.

He awoke and began to skin the animal he had gotten from the trap the night before setting the meat on the same cloth and carefully cutting the sinew that he laid carefully aside. This, he would use for the bow string; this sinew was from

the shoulder. The hide he would find use for. He took a piece of meat and, putting it on a stick, he put it over the fire. He had a lot of meat and would not be able to keep it fresh. He only planned to be in the cave a few days. After eating, he took the rest of the meat and wrapped it in some cloth and went to a nearby stream and put it in the cool water, hoping it would help to keep it fresh.

He then set off in search of something to make a bow with. He found some ash saplings and cut one, trimming the branches off. He took it back to the cave where he stripped the bark and holding it over the fire, he began to work it into shape. He cut notches in both ends and twisted the sinew into a bowstring. He strung the bow and then went in search of some thin reeds for arrows and in the mean time, he killed a bird for its feathers. He also cut it up for a meal. He set in for the night after banking the fire and slept.

Chapter Four

In the morning he woke to snow and cold; he took the clothes and put them on in layers. He still had his military socks and boots, so he rolled up the extra socks and put them in his makeshift pack. He would need snowshoes, so he went outside and cut saplings and took them into the cave to work over the fire. He bent the tips into a circle until they met the long part of the sapling about half way and then tied it with a piece of rawhide he kept in his bag. Using what was left of it, he strung it in checkerboard pattern with two loops on each to put his boots in so they would stay on.

He shouldered his pack after putting out the fire and took off after consulting his compass. He headed south, the direction he was going when he found the cave. The snowshoes were working and he was making good time when he came to a clearing and found a road. He took out the compass and taking an azimuth, he followed the road in a southeast direction. The snow wasn't as deep as it looked, so he took off the snowshoes and hung them on his back and continued on. He was going down and that was good as it meant he was going in the right direction.

He rounded a curve and saw a cabin. He hesitated, looking around to see if anyone was around it. When he saw that no one was around, he approached it carefully and found it was empty. There hadn't been anyone in it for some time. It contained a bed, stove, and a couple of buckets. He set his pack down on the bed and took a bucket and went looking for water and wood. He found water in a stream close by the cabin and filled it and took it back to the cabin and set it by the stove. He returned outside for

wood. He went around the cabin and in the rear found wood under a piece of canvas. He loaded his arms with it and returned to the cabin and started a fire in the stove. He went to the bed and unpacked the pack, taking a piece of meat and setting it on the table. He found a pan and some other canned food, mostly corn and peas, and he opened a can of corn and put it in a pot on the stove. He found a tin plate and washed it in the water along with

a fork and knife. He cooked the food and after it was ready he sat at the table and ate it. Then he banked the fire and went to bed.

He woke up and, in looking around the cabin again, he found coffee grounds. He hadn't had coffee since he was on the plane, so he made some and relaxed as he drank it. He was looking around as he drank the coffee and found another weapon: a rifle, a Winchester lever action. On further inspection, he found about twenty rounds of ammunition for it. He cleaned it and loaded it, then packed the pack and left continuing on the road. He came to a turn in the road and found a bear in the road. It looked at him and rose on its hind legs and he pumped three rounds into it, killing it.

He took out his knife and skinned it and cutting the meat, he put some in the pack. He scraped the inside of the hide and rolled it up and tied it to the pack to work on later. He continued down the road. It went uphill and rounded a corner and there was a small opening. Alongside the road, there were three or four buildings. He thumbed back the hammer on the rifle and continued on until he was in there was in the area of the buildings. All were empty and he chose the best one to stay in for a couple of nights. It would take that long for him to make the bear into something.

After putting together a fire, he takes out the map to locate where he is and found he was in an isolated town. Looking at the bottom of the map at the legend, he found he was about one hundred miles from the closest populated town and it was over rough terrain. He put some meat on the fire and began to make a coat out of the bearskin, using the deer sinew as thread and a piece of bone as a needle. After he had been working on the coat for a couple of hours, he put it aside and went to the other cabins to look around. He found some old snow shoes that were better than the ones he made, but needed some work to make them fine. He took them back to his cabin and, used some rawhide to restore them and used old belts cut to fit.his feet He tried them out and found that they fit and worked. He also used the bear coat as a blanket. It began to snow heavily. He stayed in the cabin eating the meat he had taken from the bear.

CHAPTER FIVE

On the morning of the fifth day, he packed his stuff and, putting on the snowshoes, he shot an azimuth for the direction he wanted to go and started off in that direction. The terrain was all uphill, so he cut a walking stick and started off uphill and when he reached the top of a hill, he stopped and stared in awe at the sight.

Below lay a valley with a river running through it. There were pine trees and also a number of other types and it was all covered in white; it looked like someone had laid cotton out. An elk had come to the river and was pawing at the ice to get to the water. He started down the hills and came to the valley floor and went to the river. As he got close, the elk ran off a ways and watched as he dropped his pack, took out his hatchet he found in one of the cabins, and cut a hole in the ice so the elk could get to the water. He crossed the ice to the other side and went into the trees and stopped. He watched as the elk slowly came down to the river to drink. With a smile, he turned and walked off. It was snowing again. He looked for a place to stop and found a small clearing with a lot of small saplings. He bent two of them down and, with some rawhide, he tied them. He continued this in a circle until he had the frame of a shelter. He the went to some pines and cut some boughs and, taking them back to the shelter, wove them into it until he had a shelter. There was a small hole at the top and when he built a fire, the smoke drifted out of it. He cut some more boughs for his bed and spread a couple of blankets and the bearskin over the boughs. He took some rawhide and went out and looked for animal tracks. He found rabbit tracks and set some snares and went back to the shelter to improve it.

He made some coffee with old grounds he had saved; it was strong, "boy was it strong," but it was hot and he needed it that way. In a few hours he went out to check the snares and found them full: a rabbit in each. He took them out of the snares and rolled up the pieces of rawhide and went back to his shelter.

CHAPTER SIX

He placed the rabbits on the ground and, taking his knife, skinned them. Taking a stick, he squired them and placed them over the fire as he finished his coffee. After he ate, he went outside and walked around the shelter looking for spaces in the walls; those he found he repaired with more pine. He went back inside and went to bed.

When he awoke, he restarted the fire and watched as the smoke rose up and out the hole in the roof that was made when he had tied the ends to the trees together. He pulled open the makeshift door and it was blocked with snow; it had snowed during the night. He scooped the snow away from the doorway and stood up. He took his compass and shot an azimuth, getting the direction he would go when he left.

It was still snowing and he would need food, so he took the rawhide and reset the snares and a dead fall, hoping to get something larger. He returned to the shelter and looked at the map; there was a town or city to the south. It looked to be close, but as he checked the legend at the bottom, he saw it was about fifty miles.

He put the map away and went to bed. He tucked the map under his pack and went to sleep. He woke in the cold of night; he quickly got up and restarted the fire. After he got it going and banked it, he returned to bed.

It was three days before he left. In the morning, he cleared the door, put on his bearskin coat, and went to the snares and found a couple of rabbits and in the deadfall a deer had its neck broken. He lifted the log up, pushing it away, and took his knife and began to skin it out. He took it back to the shelter and thrust some of the meat into the snow to keep it cold. He then skinned the rabbits, cooked them immediately, and ate them

He began to care for the deerskin by scraping the bits of meat off the hide he had cut and pegged and staked it down near the fire to begin to dry.

He then began to prepare the rabbit skins; he was thinking they would make a good hat with earflaps, he had enough of them. He laid the skins on the ground and, taking as piece of rawhide, he measured the size of his head and transferred it to the skins, then sewed them together with sinew from the deer. The hat fit good and he settled back to take a break, then was up packing his things.

That night after banking the fire, he slept and in the morning, he lifted the pack, put it on, picked up the rifle and in checking it, found it empty; he was out of ammunition. The rifle would be added weight, so he smashed the stock aginst a rock. He would have to rely on the bow. He took out the compass, found south, and set off in that direction.

Chapter seven

As he went on his way, he was looking for places to stay for a night or longer. He topped a hill and in the clear distance he saw a road. He took

out the binoculars and looked at the road and saw that it was paved. He had made it. He started toward the road and, in about an hour, he came to a stream. As he stopped to drink, he saw a fish jump. He set his gear down, cut a thin pole, and, using sinew, he tied a piece of deer meat to the end of the sinew and put it in the water near a fallen log. In no time, he had a bite and pulled a fish out of the water. He looked around the melted snow and saw the tops of some wild onions. He pulled them up and after cleaning the fish, he added the onion to the fish in the frying pan and cooked a small breakfast.

He watched the water for a while and then, finding a shallow place, he crossed. It was getting dark and he started looking for a place to stay for

the night and he found a place it wasn't a cave, but a place where the wind had cut a small indentation in the huge rock. It was enough to shelter

him. He set down his gear and started a fire and added more wood after the fire was going. He spread his bed out on the ground and used the bearskin coat as a blanket. He slept wishing he had some coffee. In the morning he cooked some venison for breakfast and when he was finished, he took up his gear and, putting on the coat as it was still chilly, he took out the compass again and, finding south, headed off in that direction.

He was nearing a wooded area when he saw a bear and her cubs; he froze in place and watched as they went slowly out of the woods across the open field and into the other side of the open field. He continued on his way. He found a path heading in his direction and followed it. It went along for about six miles and as it was dark, he stopped again to build a shelter, a lean-to, by cutting wood to make it. He found a tree with notches and placed two branches in them, then laid some across them and covered that with some pine boughs. He then put down his bed and slept.

In the morning, he put out the fire and set off south toward the road. He hit it about nine in the morning and as he stepped onto it, he saw a truck coming and put out his thumb. The driver stopped and asked, "Who are you?" He told him he was the only survivor of a plane crash and needed to get to the sheriff. The man asked a lot of questions, which he answered.

He was dropped off in front of the sheriff's office and, once inside, he told the sheriff of his ordeal and showed him on the map the place where he buried the others and handed over their effects. He answered all the sheriff's questions. He was released and went to a motel and fell asleep immediately and slept for two days. A knocking on the door awoke him. When he opened it he saw the relatives of the others and they asked him questions and wanted to know if anyone suffered. When he told them they didn't, the people were happy.

He called some of his friends on the phone and they were surprised to hear from him and told him they would be there to pick him up.

The end

CHALLENGE ON THE MOUNTAIN
A short Story by Art Allen

Arthur Allen

Max Miller was tired of the rat race; he had spent ten years in the Marines and wanted to get away from every thing. He

went to a surplus store and bought most of the things he would need.

He got a military sleeping bag, a military folding shovel, a hatchet, machete, sleeping mat, thermal boots for cold weather, long johns, a field jacket with a liner, a Dutch oven, a coffee pot, a frying pan, and a small sauce pan.

He went to a hardware store and bought 1,000 feet of half-inch thick rope, and an axe. He still had the knife he used in Vietnam.

It was razor sharp. He went to a dealer of off-road vehicles and bought a small, all-terrain vehicle and loaded it onto his pickup and then loaded all the other stuff on around it.

He took off for the mountains and some government land.

He came to the last town he could and after talking to the sheriff, he got permission to put his stuff in the impound area until he took care of some stuff.

He went to the local lumberman and had him build a trailer for the ATV, and then went to the local general store and saw

an old military Alice pack. This pack had places where smaller things could be attached, so he bought it and all the stuff that went with it.

He took a motel room and then found a place with maps of the mountain areas and went back to his room. Earlier in the day, he gave the guy building his trailer the phone number to his room. He was looking over the map and found a lake in the mountains and a trail to it, or so it seemed. He turned on the small radio and listened to a little country music. In the morning, he went to the store and bought a sledge hammer, buckets, blankets, and some canned food,

The lumberman called to tell him his trailer was finished.

He drove the ATV to the yard and hooked it up and went back to the impound area and loaded all of his gear onboard. He left the area and went back to the motel to get the rest of his stuff; since it was late he decided to stay one more night.

But before he left, he made one more stop at the general store.

He had seen a rifle there earlier in the day.

It was a Winchester, like the one he used in Vietnam as a sniper. He also bought a lot of ammo for it and also more ammo for the .45 caliber pistol he kept when he left the service.

He took them to his motel room and cleaned them and loaded them, then went to bed.

CHAPTER TWO

After a big breakfast of steak and eggs, he went to the impound area and started the ATV. He put the rifle in the rack on the handlebars and started out. He aimed to the mountains and throttled it on high and the ATV pulled the trailer along at a good clip.

The scenery was breathtaking and he enjoyed the ride. He turned off the road like the map said and began to climb. It was slow going and it was getting dark, so he found a place to pull over and shut off the ATV and began to set up a camp.

He took a tarp off the trailer and strung it between trees. Then he took the folding shovel and dug a pit and setting it aside, gathered wood and started a fire in the pit.

He used a little gas to start the fire and made some soup from the cans he bought from the store. He had bought a loaf of bread; it was small, but that is what he wanted. He used the bread along with the soup. When he was finished eating, he laid out his bed: the rubber sleeping mat, then the sleeping bag.

Since it was warm, he would sleep on top of it. He banked the fire and went to sleep, laying his pistol at his side.

He was up at sunrise and packed up and on the ATV and, going towards the mountain, he was on it in about three hours. When he came to *a river, he got off the vehicle and walked into the river to check on how deep it was. At this place, it was too deep, so he went along the riverbed until he found a place shallow enough to cross; he slowly crossed the river and continued on.*

He took four days to reach the place he wanted to go. He got off the ATV and went up a little hill and there he saw what he was looking for. he found the lake, it was about a mile long and half as wide. Looking through his binoculars, he slowly scanned the area. He found a small bench-like hill where he would build his cabin; he continued and saw a dark spot behind some pine trees, it could be a cave. He found a way down and went to look at it.

He could get the ATV down if he moved some rocks and trees.

He got to work and in a couple of hours he had a trail down the mountain cleared. He got on the vehicle and slowly went down the hill toward the foot of the bench. He stopped and went up the hill to look at it and decided it was what he wanted; he got back on the vehicle and went toward the cliff and stopped when he got to what was to be a cave.

He took the rifle off the handlebars and a flash light, he had taped the light under the barrel of the rifle, and went up toward the cave. The entrance was blocked by pine trees.

He slowly passed between a couple and at the entrance--

It could be the home of a bear or another animal--he stopped and passed the light across the cave and found it empty.

There had been no animals in it.

He scanned the cave and saw it would be okay to stay in it.

He went to the ATV and lay the rifle down on the vehicle and

put the pistol on his belt then began to unload the trailer, carrying all the things into the cave. It took him a couple of hours to unload the trailer and arrange his gear the way he wanted it.

He laid the sleeping mat at the back of the cave and the sleeping bag on it.

He stacked all the other stuff to the side and went to get some wood. He stacked stones to form a fireplace and built a fire using a little gas to start it. While the fire was getting started, he opened a can of beef stew and poured it into the small frying pan, then took out the coffee pot and poured grounds in the water and set it on the side of the fire.

When he finished eating, he went to the small bench where he would build his cabin. He paced out the outline of the building.

But for now, he needed to make the cave livable, as he would be there for a time. He put out the fire and then hooked up the trailer and went to the river where he scooped some mud into the trailer. Close to the cave he cut grass to make a substance to hold stones together; he put a fireplace together and looked up to see a crack in the roof. He went up on top of the hill and found a bush covered the crack. That would disperse the smoke.

On the way back down the mountain, he found a hollow log and decided it would make a good chimney for the fireplace to the roof. He held it in place and used the mud to hold it in place; the heat from the fire would harden the mud.

To his surprise, it worked. Next, he used the wooden box the food came in as a table.

Next, he needed to find a way to keep the wind out when winter came; the trees weren't close enough together to stop the wind. He decided he would have to go back to town to get something and that would be in the beginning of the week. In the mean time he planned to break up rocks to begin building his cabin. He took the sledgehammer and went to the hill and began breaking up rocks.

These he was going to use to build his cabin. It was early spring and he took off his windbreaker and shirt and began again to hammer at the rocks. He would hammer for about an hour, then move the stones nearer to the hill where he was going to put his cabin.

He had been at it for about four hours when he took a break and heard a whining from the nearby woods. He holstered his .45 and slowly advanced toward the sound. He passed the tree *line and saw a wolf lying on her side. She was dead, most likely the result of a fight with another animal. The whine came from his rear. He turned and saw a wolf pup; it was under a bush and trembling.*

"Hey, little guy. Your mom is dead. I'll take you and lookout for you," he grabbed the cub by the skin in the back and lifted it. He took it to the cave. He opened a can of milk and poured it into a pan and the cub drank up.

The cub stuck around and followed him around as he worked at the site; he had been there a month when he realized he was running out of food and other stuff. He hooked up the trailer and put his rifle in the hooks at the handlebars, tucked the cub in a cage he had made, and took off for the town. That night he stopped at the place he did on his way up the mountain. He let the cub out and he threw a piece of meat to it and started a fire to cook his dinner, and then he went to bed. The cub snuggled next to him and slept.

He pulled into town and went to the sheriff's office and checked with him, then to the store where he bought ten 50-pound bags of cement and more ammo for both weapons. He picked up a couple of cooler chests and ice and put some meat in them; this he would use until he could kill some meat. He also bought a lot of canned fruit, salt, sugar, and flour. He went to the lumberyard and got some 2x4s and nails and spikes. He loaded it all.

As he was loading, a child got to close to the cub and it nipped at him, but it didn't hurt him just scared him. The kid's dad was going to shoot the cub. Max told the man, "You shoot it, and I'll shoot you," and he got on the ATV and left.

CHAPTER THREE

He took off at a fast pace and didn't look back. As he neared the turn off, he took it slowly so the load wouldn't tip. At his camp place, he took the cub out of his cage and set him down.

He spoke to it, "I'm gonna have to name you boy. I'll think of it soon." The cub stopped and looked at Max and its tail wagged.

As he built his fire he said, "Boy, your name is Flame. Here, Flame." The cub came to him; he scratched it behind its ear and began to make his meal. He cut some meat from what he bought in the store, opened a can of vegetables, emptying it into a pan and sit back to let it cook.

He thought as he ate of things he could do to the cabin.

He looked down and saw Flame looking at him; he took a piece of meat and put it in front of him. Flame sniffed it and looked at him, then he turned and went into the woods. He was gone for a while; when he came back, Max knew he had been hunting, "Okay, Flame, you do your thing and I won't interfere, but you stay around." He banked the fire and went to bed. he had bought some books while in town and now he began to read one. It

was a western. He liked them and had gotten about five for now.

He was into it a couple of pages when Flame came in. There was a little blood around his mouth and he went to the bucket that had a little water left and drank. When he had finished, he slowly walked over and lay down next to Max and slept. Max marked the page and turned down the lamp and went to sleep.

In the morning he made coffee and had a little breakfast, then went back to breaking up rocks and moving them to the hill. He returned to the cave and while eating, he was looking

around and thought that it was getting close to winter and he had better get ready. The first thing he would have to do was figure a way to keep the wind out. He thought of all the trees

at the base of the hills and after lunch he went to the woods with an axe and began to cut down trees. He dragged them to the cave and, with the hatchet, he trimmed them to fit the mouth of the cave.

He lashed the poles together and wedged them into the front of the cave; he then cut a piece of the tarp to fit the doorway.

He weighted it down with stones, thus holding it in place. He waited until it was dark, lit the lamp, then went outside and looked in. He would fill in the cracks with mud in the morning.

In the morning, he mixed the mud and patched the cracks with it. This would also keep some animals out.

He took from the small trailer the bags of cement, a shovel he had bought the last time he was in town, and the bucket and went to the lake and filled it. On returning to the hill, he mixed it until it was as it was supposed to be, opened one of the bags of cement, and poured it into the trailer, then added some dirt and water

He went to the hill and began laying out the stones along the marks he had made. Then putting cement on them, he laid a second layer of stones, then a layer of cement. He continued this until he had the wall waist high; then he quit for the day.

He went to the cave, got some soap and a change of clothes and a towel and headed for the lake. Flame followed. He stripped and went into the water, soaped down, and then dove under and rinsed off. He lifted Flame into the water and washed him off. The wolf at first fought, then settled down when Max began to soap him down.

When he had finished Flame, he left the water and dried off and dressed, then dried Flame off, who then, just like an animal, rolled in the dirt. Max knew it was inbred in the wolf and just shook his head as he headed back to the cave, and dinner.

While he was preparing his dinner, he heard a gushing sound and, after dinner, began to explore the cave. He really had not done this before.

He took a lamp and headed toward the back of the cave.

He found a hole in the floor and dropped a stone, counting

the time it took the stone to hit water. He calculated it was

about twenty feet down. He went to the front, got a bottle and some string he had bought, and tying the string around the neck of the bottle, he lowered it until he could feel resistance, then slowly pulled it back up.

The bottle was cold when he touched it and when he took a sip, it was cold and good. He decided it would be his refrigerator. He needed a box with holes in it and decided that the next time he went to town, he would get a couple of the crates that milk men use to deliver their milk.

He finished his dinner and found that he was out of coffee, looked like it was going to be in the morning that he would go to town. In the morning he hooked up the trailer and headed for town with Flame trotting alongside. In two days, as they came close to town, Flame stopped and trotted off the trail.

Max stopped and said, "What is wrong, boy?" The wolf looked at him and Max thought for a minute and remembered the last time they went to town. "Okay, fella, you wait here. I won't be long."

CHAPTER FOUR

While he was in town, he asked the storeowner for a couple of the boxes he was thinking about. The man gave him three and he picked up some more food and meat this time

He returned to the ATV and placed the stuff in the trailer.

When he remembered the saw, he went back to the store and got two, a regular saw and a crosscut saw, then he returned

to the ATV and started it. As it idled, he returned again to the store for a couple of pencils and some paper.

He was off. At the regular camping spot he started a fire and put some meat on and made coffee. As he waited for it all to cook, he took out the paper and a pencil and began to sketch what he wanted to do to the cabin and the ideas

from his head.

He had planned to cut some trees and notch the logs so they interlocked after shaving one side smooth with the sharp machete. He figured 3 logs the length of the cabin and shorter

one the width of the cabin, all notched to fit, and to use the spikes to hold them together. He would cut the 2x4s for windows and doorways.

He planned to make the fireplace like a box, three sides on the inside, and it would be wide and high enough to stand in. After he had finished the meal, he had given a little of the canned meat to Flame and the animal turned his nose up at it.

"Okay, go and get your own," and with that the wolf/dog went into the woods.

Max shook his head and smiled as he went back to the fire.

He refilled his coffee cup and sat back to think about the future, the near future. In about half an hour, Flame came back. Max noticed a little blood at his mouth and knew he had been hunting, "Oh, you got something to eat huh, fella?" The animal wagged its tail and went to a nearby stream and stuck his muzzle in to clean it off.

Max went to bed and Flame lay down next to him and they went to sleep. In the morning they were up with the sun, packed and on their way. A few days later they went down into the valley and the cave. As Max unloaded the trailer, Flame went off to explore his territory. After unloading the trailer, Max carried a couple of cement bags to the cabin site and began to mix up a batch and began to build the lower section of the fireplace

In about two hours he had the chimney to the edge of the

wall that he had built. He figured out how big he wanted the windows and began to cut the 2x4s for them and the doorway.

He would have to cut a couple of logs to go over the windows and door to support the weight.

THE TRANSPARENT DETECTIVE

While he was at the cutting, he cut the logs for the floor. They would all be about six inches in diameter. After he cut them, he used the sharp machete to square off one side of each log. He

then placed them in place, three lengthwise and six wide. He

had notched the bottom of the short logs and fitted them perfectly to the long ones. He had looked around and found a slab of rock and, using the sledgehammer, he trimmed it and laid it on the floor at the place where the fireplace would be.

He cut and lay some logs. After trimming them over the windows and doors, the sun was setting. He decided he would go for a swim in the lake and stripped down and, taking his soap, jumped in. He heard a splash and turned to see Flame swimming, too. After a short swim, he washed and then dried as he started for the cave. He heard a roar coming from the woods and ran for the cave. He snatched up his rifle and headed for the woods toward the roar.

He was moving quickly toward it and stopped quickly. There,

in a small clearing, was a grizzly bear fighting with two wild cats. A cub barely old enough to move was hiding under a log. The cats were getting the best of the bear. It was down and the cats killed it and were after the cub. He raised the rifle and killed first one, then the other of the cats.

He took the cub and went back to the cave, put it in a box with a blanket, then went back and skinned the adult bear and cats; he could use the bear skin and he needed meat. He took it all back to the cave and, removing the cub from the box, he tied a rope to the corners and then another piece to the middle. Placing meat in the box, he lowered the box to the river that ran beneath the cave. He pulled it up to make sure the meat was wet and lowered it again and tied it off. He went to bed and slept good.

CHAPTER FIVE

He woke to a sound that was like someone in trouble and found the cub was hungry.

He pulled up one of the boxes and took some milk out of it and mixed it with meat and fed the cub. He figured it was about a year old and could fend for itself if it had to. He put it back in the box and carried it to the cabin site, where he let it out. The cub and Flame began to play together. He smiled and began to work.

By the end of the day he had three more rows of stone laid

and was in the mood for a swim. The cub and Flame were in the water already and playing. Max went in and the animals came to him to play; they played for about an hour, then went back to the cave.

On the way back to it, he noticed it was getting colder and knew that he would have to put off working on the cabin

until spring and would have to go to town to stock up on some food if he could get there.

When he awoke in the morning, he found it was cold. Looking outside, he saw snow and knew he was in trouble for the time being. He started a fire and looked in on the animals; they were ok. He dressed in long johns, a wool shirt, baseball cap, and gloves. He went out to see how the ATV was and it was covered with snow. He covered it with a tarp after brushing off the snow.

He would have to buy a snowmobile when he went to town the next time. He went back into the cave made breakfast. He pulled up the box in which he had stored the meat and cut off a piece. He opened a can of corn and boiled the meat and corn and made coffee. After he ate, he took the bear cub outside and let it play in the snow with Flame while he went down to the cabin to look and see if the snow did any damage. It had not, so he went back to the cave followed by the bear and Flame.

He sat and began the task of scraping the excess skin off the bear hide of the bear. He thought it would make a rug in the cabin. He scraped the loose skin off the hide and rolled it up; he would stretch it in the spring. He walked back to the cave followed by the animals. He made his dinner and as the animals settled down, he took out a book and began to read.

He was halfway through the book when he felt funny.

He put the book down and went to a box and dug out a legal pad and began to write. He had gone through half of the pad when he laid his head on the makeshift table.

CHAPTER SIX

The spring sun topped the mountain as four figures topped the mountain: the sheriff and three others, one a game warden or park ranger, the others deputies. The sheriff looked through the binoculars and saw the half-finished cabin.

He saw movement and turned in that direction; there was the bear, now almost full-grown, playing with a wolf-dog.

The party started down the mountain and the animals took off running toward the cave. They stopped and began to growl

as the people came closer. The animals began to growl, the

bear was on his hind legs, mouth open, the wolf-dog was growling. One of the deputies drew his weapon, but the sheriff held out his hand. The park ranger took out a tranquilizer gun, loaded it, and shot the bear, then reloaded and shot the wolf.

After the drug took effect, the sheriff went into the cave.

"Oh, damn, no." He went to the makeshift table. There, slumped over the table, was the body of Mike. He had a yellow legal pad and the last sentence told the sheriff what happened: "I knew it would happen sometime my heart is giving out." The sheriff took the pad and read it, it was all the chapters above, and it asked the finder to see that his land here be given to his next of kin and that his animals be turned loose as they could fend for themselves.

With the help of the others, the sheriff sewed Mike's body into a piece of canvas and loaded it onto the trailer and drove it to the cabin. There, on small hill behind the cabin, they buried Mike.

They carved out a cross and placed it at the head of the grave.

It said, "Here lies Mike Miller He lost the challenge on the mountain."

They took off and, as they topped the mountain, they heard a howling and, looking through his binoculars, the sheriff saw the animals at the grave; the bear lay on it and the wolf was also laying at the foot of it.

Mike Miller has lost the challenge on the mountain; he had been there two years.

THE END

THE RIDE OF MAC HANSEN

Arthur Allen

CHAPTER 1

The crickets and caddies had quit their serenade and the sun was just peeping about the hills. The black dog lifted its massive head and growled, got to its feet, and moved off into the twilight. The man rolled out of his bedroll, grabbed his Winchester, and levered it, chambering a round.

A shadow moved near his horses and he fired at it. The figure went down and the dog let at another and they went down, the Indian yelling as the dog's teeth sank into his throat. Another one fired into the bed as Mac rolled to the right and fired at the remaining Indian, bringing him down with a shot to the chest. The Indian was knocked back into the bush.

Mac stood and looked around as he heard the sound of receding hoofbeats. The dog came out of the trees, blood on its mouth, and went to the nearby river to drink and clean its face. Mac checked the bodies and found that each had a new 20-dollar gold piece. He pocketed them. Looks like someone is trying to stop me, he thought, as his mind raced back to the beginning of this ride.

It all began in Missouri, outside of Sedalia, on a farm. He had gone to town to get some groceries. When he came home, he found his mother, father, sister, and young wife dead. He sat there, stunned, and cried. At age 21, his world had ended. The next day he buried his folks and then went to town to report it to the sheriff, who he knew would do nothing. He returned to the farm and, taking his father's weapons, he began to practice, and practice and practice. He kept at it until he was so accurate, he could hit a penny at 50 yards with a rifle and hit all the spots on a card at 20 paces after a fast draw. He had a 44 caliber in a holster tied down and another in his belt.

He heard a sound and, drawing, spun around to see a dog whining and limping into the yard. He went to the dog and it snarled as he came closer. "Easy, boy, I'm not gonna hurt you," he said softly and the dog quieted down and Mac looked at the wounds.

A whip and club had made them. He bathed the wounds and bound them and fed the dog. He made a place for the animal in the house.

In about a week the dog was well and was hunting on his own, but he always came back to Mac. In another week, he saddled up his horse and got his dad's money from the hiding place in the fireplace, which came to 500 dollars and was missed by the killers. He went to town to the sheriff and told him that he was going after the men who killed his family, then to the family lawyer to arrange to sell the farm. He told the lawyer he'd keep in touch and to send the money to the address he would send when the time came.

CHAPTER 2

He rode out of town a year to the day he found his folks dead and with a lead on where he could find some of the men. He went into the next town and bought a packhorse; he also got a shotgun and supplies. As he left the store, a man was trying to steal his horse and the dog was snapping at him. The man drew his gun to shoot the dog and Mac drew and shot the man in the arm. Mac said, "You're lucky I didn't kill you, mister." With that, he mounted and said, "Come on, dog, let's go," and the animal trotted off after him. He headed west to Kansas, to Colorado, where in the town of Trinidad he met up with the first of the men he was looking for in the saloon. He went in for a beer and two of the men who killed his family were there. One of them said, "Hey, you look like Hans Hansen."

"Yes. I'm his son and looking for the men who killed him and the rest of my family."

The man went for his piece, but he died even as his gun cleared leather. Mac's shots sounded like one and both men lay on the floor in sawdust and blood.

The sheriff ran in and wanted to know what happened. When the people told him, he told Mac, "Okay, it was self-defense, but leave town now. I don't want you around here."

Mac said, "I'll go when my business here is finished and not before. These men killed my family and they are just two. I'll find the rest and they will pay. He slowly walked out the door and mounted and rode to the general store where he bought some shotgun shells. He left the store and mounted his horse and they left town.

He made camp on a stream bank that evening and had just settled in when he heard a noise and ducked as a bullet whipped past his head. He rolled toward a bush was up and running in the direction of the shot when he saw a man getting on a horse. He drew and fired and hit the man. He fell to the ground and Mac was on him. the man was wounded and had lost his pistol. Mac asked him as he put a foot

on the wound, "Who sent you after me?"
and pressed on the wound.

The man yelled out and told Mack he
didn't know he contacted him by
mailwhere he could be found, "He's in
Wyoming, a town called Rock Springs. He's
a lawyer there. He wanted your wife and
when she wouldn't go with him, he killed
her and the rest of your family. He was
mad when he couldn't find you and he
heard from Missouri that you were on the
way. He sent me out to stop you, but I
didn't think you were this good." Those
were his last words as he died there.

CHAPTER 3

Mac buried the man, then saddled his horse and headed forRock Springs. On the way he stopped by a little spring and in the early dawn was attacked by Indians. He buried them and, as the dog came to him, he noticed that he had been cut, so he went to the pack horse and got some medical stuff and took care of the cut. It wasn't deep, but it bled he had to cauterize it and the dog yelped when the hot metal touched his side and he snapped at Mac's hand.

"Easy, dog. I had to do that it will be okay."

The dog

seemed to understand and licked his hand. He patted the dog on the head and went to the packhorse and put the stuff away and mounted and turned to head for Rock Springs, Wyoming. He had been on the trail for three days when he came on a wagon with a family. The wheel was broken and the man was trying to replace it, but having a hard time of it.

He asked, "Having a hard time?"

The man said, "Yes, I am."

Mac offered to help. He got down from the horse and went to a tree and, using his Bowie, he cut a small tree and moved to the wagon. He moved a cut stump near the wheel and told the man, "When I lift, you slide the stump under the axle." He grunted and put all his weight on it and the wagon rose high enough to do the job. When the wheels were changed and the wagon lowered, Mac went to his horse.

The man spoke, "Mister, my name is Josh Kinder and this is my wife, Irene, and my son, Joe. We would like it if you stayed and had supper with us."

Mac saw the boy edging toward the dog, "Joe, don't touch the dog. He doesn't like most people." With that, the dog went to the boy and licked his hand and the boy's face lit up like it was the best thing that ever happened to him.

He asked Mac, "What's his name?"

Mack looked bewildered and laughed, "He doesn't have one. I call him Dog and he seems happy with it."

Irene said, "Supper is ready. Please sit."

Mac had the best meal he had had in a long time said so and was thanked with a smile. "So where are you going?" he asked.

"We were part of a wagon train that was heading for Oregon and the wheel broke. We were told to meet them at a river nearby and they'll wait for us. We will leave in the morning."

Mack told them he would stay the night and go with them to the river, "This is Indian country. Although there aren't many around, there are still some."

He took his bedroll and rolled it out under some trees a ways from the wagon; the dog lay near him and he lay thinking who was this guy who killed his family. First, he had to find out who it is and he had to be careful because this guy knew he was looking for him. He had sent out a gunman to kill him. The guy said he knew he left Missouri, so it had to be some one else was involved and that someone else is in the town near his home.

He drifted off to sleep and came awake to the sound of someone nearby. He came up with his gun in his hand, cocked and ready, when he saw Joe and the dog close by. "Boy, don't sneak up on people like that," he said.

"I'm sorry! I wanted to pet the dog before we left," the boy moaned, his eyes wide as he stared at the gun as Mac eased the hammer down and put it away.

He began to roll up his bedroll and put it behind his saddle after he saddled buck the horse side stepped and Mack packed the packhorse and led the animals to the wagon where he could smell breakfast. As he tied the horses to the wagon, he looked at the fire and exclaimed, "Eggs! I haven't had eggs in quite a while!"

Irene handed him a plate and he ate with gusto and had two cups of coffee. They left for the river and made it at sundown. The family was greeted by the others. As they looked at him and asked the Kinders who he was, a man came up to him and said, "You better go, mister, we don't want your kind here."

Mac asked, "What is my kind?"

The man said, "A gunfighter."

"What makes you think I'm a gunfighter?" Mac asked.

"Your gun is tied down," the man replied.

"Where are you from?" Mac asked.

"I don't think it is your business," he scowled. Mac brushed by him and the man grabbed Mac's arm. Mac spun, and like lighting, his fist connected with the man's jaw and he dropped like a brick. Mack continued toward the fire when a shout made him turn and he drew as he did and fired. The bullet hit the ax handle the man had picked up and he yelped and grabbed his hand. The bullet had hit the handle an inch above his hand, causing splinters to go into his hand.

He holstered his weapon and asked Josh, "Who was that?"

Josh told him, "I don't know," and turned to ask an older bearded man.

"He is a man who joined us three days ago. He is trying to take over. He and his men have bullied us from the start."

Mac went to the man's wagon and told him, "Get out of here or else."

The man growled, "Or else what? You'll kill us?"

Mac smiled and said, "Yes, I will if you continue to bother these people. I know who you are. I wasn't sure until I saw him." Mac nodded to a thin man standing by the wagon his hands hooked in his belt. He had a sly grin on his face. Mack told him, "Ringo, if you go for that gun, I'll kill you."

Ringo smiled a wicked smile and said, "You never saw the day you could beat me, nobody can. I'M the best," and with that, he drew. His gun just cleared leather and he jerked as the bullets hit him.

The shots were like one and the speed with which he drew amazed the others as he swung his gun to cover them.

"Don't even think of it."

Their hands were poised at their guns.

"Get on your wagon and leave now and I'll stay with these people for a while, so don't think about coming back." He stood and watched as they hooked up the horses to their wagon and moved out. He turned and saw that every man in the wagon train had a gun in his hand, he knew they were with him.

A man walked up to him and said, "Mr. Hansen I'm, Matt Hanks, the wagon master, and I want to thank you for that. We all were afraid they would shoot us. You can stay with us as long as you want."

He thanked them and told them he had to go; he was looking for some one and needed to go.

In the morning, he saddled up and he and the dog trotted off, headed north for the man who could answer his questions, questions that have been nagging him.

Who is the man who wanted his family dead? He had gone, maybe ten miles, when he heard a horse coming and moved off the trail to see who it was and was surprised to see one of the men he had run off from the train and he was moving fast.

Mack decided to follow him and pushed Buck onto the trail and followed the man. He had a clue to where the man was going, a town called Lander, but he followed the man to a small ranch outside Lander. He pulled off the trail and dismounted and got his binoculars from his saddlebag. He moved behind a rock and looked toward the ranch. He focused

on the man who was getting off his horse,
when the door to
   the house opened and a man came out.

CHAPTER 4

Mac was shocked at first, but when he stopped to think about it, the sheriff of his town had been rumored to be crook and this might prove it.

He moved closer and ended at the corner of the house. The trees and bushes went right to there.

He could hear what they were saying, "He ran us off from the wagon train. He is fast with that gun and killed my brother, Mike."

The sheriff told him, "Well, then, that gives you a reason to kill him doesn't it?"

The outlaw asked him, "Why do you want him dead, anyway?"

"There is gold on that farm, but his father was too dumb to find it.

I offered him a price for his farm. He refused and I had tried to run them off, but they fought back, so I had them killed and got the gold anyway."

Mack stood and moved to the men. The man he had been following saw him first.

"Oh, damn," he went for his gun.

Mack killed him and the sheriff threw up his hands, "I'm not armed! Don't shoot!" he cried out and Mac hit him, knocking him to the ground.

As he moved to the sheriff, a shot rang out and he felt it hit his leg.

As he went down, he turned and shot at the shadow in the doorway and saw it go down. His gun moved to cover the sheriff as he moved to get up. "Just hold it there, Sheriff," and he got up. His leg hurt, but it was a crease and not bad. "Let's go see who shot at me," he said and followed the sheriff to the house. On the floor lay a man.

He had been shot in the chest and as Mac bent down to check his pulse, the sheriff made his move and kicked at Mac. He lifted the barrel of his gun an inch and fired. The bullet hit the sheriff in the knee and he grabbed it and screamed as he fell to the floor.

"You never learn, do you Herb?" Herbert was the sheriff's first name.

"I'm taking you back to Missouri and you'll hang for the murders of my family."

The sheriff said as he gripped his damaged knee, "You don't have the authority to arrest me." Mike grinned at him and, holstering his gun, he reached into his

shirt and pulled out a big wallet. From it, he pulled a piece of paper and handed it to Herb and said, "Read it."

As Herb read it, his jaw dropped and Mike pinned on a U.S.

Marshal's badge on his vest.

Herb looked up and saw the badge, "When did this happen?"

Mike smiled and said, "It happened four days ago at the wagon train. Stop at fort miller there was a u.s. marshal there and he swore me in as a deputy marshal ,

He was also after you.

I killed these two for the murders I was after you for."

Herb confessed, "Well, I hope you are good because you wont get me back."

Mac told him, "I'll get you back sitting in your saddle or laying across it, but I'll get you back. Now let's get you to a doctor."

In the nearby town, the sheriff was asking questions and Mike showed him his badge and told him about the murders and the swearing in. The doctor fixed Herb's knee and after a few days rest, they left for

Missouri, only they took the stagecoach with Buck tied on the back and the dog running alongside. Mac wanted to put the dog on top, but he wanted to run. When they stopped, Mac looked for dog and petted him every chance he got. He had cuffed Herb and the other passengers looked at him like he was what he was, a killer.

After four days on the stagecoach, they arrived in the town of Sedalia, which was where they started. As they got down from the stage, the new sheriff came up to Mac and asked, "Marshal Hansen?"

Mac looked at him and said, "Yes, and I've got the former sheriff here. He's wanted for murder and I arrested him. I want him locked up right now and a guard put on him. He has friends who may try to break him out of jail."

They escorted Herb to the jail and locked him in a cell. Then mike asked, "Herb, who was in this with you? You aren't smart enough to pull this off yourself and I want to know if you have registered the gold on my land."

Herb smiled, "You don't really expect me to answer that do you?"

Mac grinned and said, "So there is someone else."

At the same time they came into town, the banker and a lawyer were in the bank and saw them arrive. The banker said, "Oh, no. Look at that. Herb under arrest and look who is wearing a badge."

The lawyer looked and said, "Damn. We're in trouble.

I saw him in Colorado and he is a terror with that gun, but I didn't know he was a Marshal."

The banker said, "We can kill him. I'M not gonna lose that mine. It's mine."

The lawyer said, "No, it's ours," and was amazed at the look of a mad man in the banker's eyes.

The banker went into his office and as the lawyer came in, the banker hit him on the head with a club. When he hit the floor, he hit him again and again. It was dark, so he would have no trouble getting the body out of the building. He wrapped the body in the carpet that covered the floor and went to get a wagon, in which he loaded the body.

He then drove out of town and when he was three miles out, he unrolled the carpet and dumped the lawyer's body on the ground. He went through the pockets, turning them inside out. He took the belongings and put them in his pocket, then drove back towards town, where he stopped at a ditch where he put the body and burned it. He then drove back to town and went to bed.

At the same time he was loading the lawyer's body in the wagon, one of the town drunks was watching. When the wagon had gone, he went to the sheriff's office and reported it. Mac was there as he had established an office there and he listened as the man told him what he had seen. He thanked the man and went to bed.

At sunup, he was in the saddle and he had an extra horse. He headed out of town and found the body of the lawyer. He had to fire his gun in the air because the buzzards were already there. When the buzzards left, he went to the body and rolled it over. A wave of nausea came over him as he noticed that the buzzards had gone for the eyes first. He loaded the body on the horse and started to town. The smoke from the rug caught his eye, and as he rode up to it, he noticed it wasn't all burned and there was still blood on it.

He took all this back to town and left it with the doc, then he went through town asking questions and checking records and facts. He went to the restaurant and had lunch. As he drank coffee, he watched the town and thought. He stopped suddenly and got up paid for the meal, went out to the livery stable, saddled his horse, and went out of town to his old farm. It was deserted and he went in and to the fireplace.

He looked for and found the loose stone and worked at it until it came free.

Behind it, he found a metal strongbox. He replaced the stone and left the house.

As he stepped out on the porch, he noticed the dog was standing stiff-legged and growling. He threw himself to the left as a bullet hit the wall where he was standing and rolled off the porch as shots followed him. He rounded the corner and got to his horse. He pulled his Winchester from its scabbard and threw the butt into his shoulder had fired at the small hill where the shots had come from. He heard a cry and took off in that direction. He got there in time to see a horse galloping toward town.

He recognized the horse and went back to the house. He said, "Dog, find," and the hound trotted off, his muzzle to the ground. The dog headed toward the hill and sniffed around, then trotted off in the direction the horse took.

CHAPTER 5

The dog stopped for a while at a stream and Mac got down and looked toward where the dog was. He went there and squatted there. He saw some blood spots.

The dog crossed the stream and headed for town.

An hour later, they came into town at a walk. The dog went straight to the banker's house. Mac dismounted and took his gun out and went up the stairs. He knocked at the door and when the banker opened it, he saw the gun.

Mac told him, "You are under arrest for the murder of lawyer Sam Hawks and my family."

The banker
laughed and said, "You dumb man, you can't prove it."

Mac grinned and said, "There was a witness to the murder. Someone saw you load the body into the wagon and
I have the motive in my saddlebags, let's go." As Mac turned, the dog leaped at the banker. Mac turned to see the dog on the

man's chest, his mouth at the man's throat. In his hand was a knife.

"Stop, dog," Mac said, and the dog backed off. The Marshal took the knife and slid it in his belt, jerked the banker to his feet and applied a set of cuffs.

As he locked the cell he said, "You didn't look in the fireplace. I have the mineral rights here in the box and my dad hid them there, so you killed them for nothing.

The gold is and has always been mine."

The banker reached through the bars as he screamed, "Noooooooooooooooooo"

Mac stepped back and smiled, "You'll be in there until the circuit judge comes, then you go on trial for murder."

Mike left the office and went to the assayer office to register his gold mine.

The assayer said, "It should assay out at two hundred dollars a ton. You're gonna be a rich man, Marshal."

"Thanks," he said, as he took the paper and left.

Mac resigned from the marshal's job and moved back to the farm, which is now one of the biggest ranches in Missouri. He has land in the west and is planning to drive cows west instead east to a new ranch he is building there.

He still keeps his hand in as a gun handler and the dog is still with him, although he's a lot older. Mike just couldn't put him down, the dog rides in the wagon on padded blankets and is fed by a man hired especially to take care of him, although he
a girl friend and puppies.

It is a happy time for him; all he needs now is a woman to make it complete.

THE END

Arthur Allen

ODYESSY OF THE DRAGON

This is not a story of the type of dragon that were mythical creatures of old,
that terrorized the people. It does not fly, it does not spit fire, and it doesn't have a long
tail. It is the story of a tank and its crew, of their affection for this piece of metal with a life of its own.

Arthur Allen

CHAPTER ONE

The tank was squatting on the cement slab that is known to the tankers as the Tank Park.

It was forest green with some rust spots and a lot of dirt. The turret was covered with a tarp.

The turret was to the rear. The bottom portion of a letter "b" and numbers 34 could be seen

below the tarp.

The crew Sergeant Mike Johnson, the gunner Corporal Mat Norman, the driver Corporal Johnny Dole,

the loader Jimmy Willis, all stood looking at this monster.

Sergeant Johnson said, "Okay, men.

Let's get the tarp off. I know all of you have been through tank school and know what to do.

I'll be here to answer any questions." The crew jumped on the tank and began to untie the

tarp and pulled it off. The sergeant threw a key to Corporal Norman, who unlocked the turret and pulled the loaders hatch open.

The crew climbed in.

"Holy shit! What a mess!" the corporal yelled and the other two looked in.

"Man, look at all that dirt and mud," groaned Willis.

"We will have to clean it up," Sergeant. Johnson

said as he climbed on the tank. "Want the best section in the company and that means that both this tank and 35 will be clean and all maintenance done. Norman, you and Willis start to clean

the turret. Dole, you clean the driver's compartment. I'll help wherever it is needed."

The men

went to work and began to clean the tank up. Sergeant Johnson slowly walked around it, looking at

the suspension system; it looked pretty bad, a lot of the rubber was torn off, the road wheels and

a lot of trackblocks were worn.

It took about a week to clean it up and upon inspection, all but the track and wheels were clean. The crew began to work on the track. First, they broke it by removing the tension by use

of the track adjusting wrench. When the track was slack, the end connectors, which hold the

track together, along with the center guides, which were removed first, were knocked off with the use of a crowbar and sledgehammer. The track was then strung out

and the damaged blocks replaced in the same way. Then the track was attached together and the

damaged road wheels were removed with a type of jack, which was placed on an arm on the rear

of all the wheels. The vehicle was moved so the wheel was up off the track, then it was replaced

in the same way; all wheels were removed two at a time if necessary. The same went for

the support rollers, of which there were five on each side that were removed differently.

The crew was finishing up a paint job on the vehicle when the platoon leader came to Mike and said, "We have permission to name the vehicles."

The crew got together to try to name

it. Later that week, the platoon was on a driving mission to evaluate the crew on tactics and, as

a break from the day's work on an old stretch of highway, the vehicles were drag racing.

Mike Johnson's tank beat all the tanks in the company, so the crew agreed that the name of

the tank should be the "Dragon wagon" and that was stenciled on its guntube.

The following week, the crew went to the field to practice their gunnery. At hill 409,

which is the gunnery range at Pendleton, the company lined up the tanks and the crews

began to get ready. Mike instructed his people on how to boresight the gun and sights of

the dragon. While the loader was taping string across the end of the barrel, Mike and Mat removed the percussion mechanism, the name given the firing pin of the 90 mm

gun. Once that was removed, Mat got into his gunner's seat and Mike, putting the binoculars against the hole, left by the pin lined up the crosshair on the end of the guntube on the upper right

corner of a target with straight edges. Then, all the sights were put on the same place, by use of

ther elevation and traversing handles

The firing pin is replaced and the vehicle loaded with ammo. The loader places the 90mm ammo in the apporite racks. In the ready racks for his easy access, he also loads the

30-caliber machine gun, mounted on the left of the main gun and used primarily

for the engagement of infantry and marking targets. The commander, Sergeant Johnson, also bore

and sighted his 50 caliber machine gun on the target.

CHAPTER TWO

The firing began by zeroing the weapons by putting the cross hair of the gun and sights
on the target and fire a three round group they then by using the knobs on the sight put the
cross hair in the center of that three round shot group. A final zeroing shot is fired, it should hit where the sights were put.

The thirty caliber is sighted by a red circle in the gunner's sight when the gun is fired. When the tracer rounds seem to pass through the center of the red circle, it is on the target. The
command to fire comes from the range officer and Sergeant Johnson yells, "Gunner h.e. bunker."

At this time, he places the turret in the general area of the target. The gunner does the final lay and yells, "Identified!"

The loader loads an h. e. round and yells, "Up!" Sergeant Johnson commands, "Fire!"

Mat presses the firing button on his control. The cannon fires, the breech comes back 12 to 13 inches and as it moves back, the empty casing is ejected from the breech and the loader loads another round and the gunner fires. The target is gone and Mike yells, "Cease fire!"

The loader begins to throw the empty brass shells out of his hatch. He yells, "Brass!" and throws it out. The spent brass from the machine gun is caught in a canvas bag that has a zipper on the bottom.

The ammo capacity of the tank is 64 rounds of 90mm ammo, 36000 rounds of 30-caliber

ammo, 5000 rounds of ammo, and about 1000 rounds of.45 caliber ammo for the crew's personal weapons. Each man carried a .45 caliber automatic and the commander had a .45 caliber

submachine gun at his disposal.

After the cease-fire, the range officer would tell the crews to fire machine guns or something

else. In the turret, the gunner sat on the right front with the commander behind him andslightly above the loader, who sat on the left rear, with ammo behind him and in front of him.

Besides his loading duties, he also took care of the vehicle's radios, called the a.n.g.r.c-3,

which stood for army, navy ground receiver type 3. He would set the frequency and clean them.

On the turret wall to the commander's right was the instrument to operate the tank's

18-inch searchlight. This light was used to illuminate the target at night, or used in

the flicker method, in which one tank illuminates the target and the other

shoots, then the one that fired lights the target and the one that first lit the target then fires.

All five tanks were fitted with the 18 inch light until the xenon light came along, then only

three tanks in the platoon would carry a light. The xenon was also infrared for night use.

The gunner was equipped with an infrared sight that was incorporated into his gunner's sight.

The type of ammo for the 90 mm gun is varied; it can carry AP, or armor piercing ammunition; A.p.d.c.,

Armor piercing discarding sabot; Hep, high explosive plastic; he., High explosive; W.p., white

phosphor smoke; and canisters, which contain 1200 38 caliber pellets used

against personnel. Canisters looked like a giant shotgun shell. It was later changed to the flashette,

which contains 4400 steel dartsand has a fuse that could be set to go off at various ranges.

Depending upon the intelligence, the unit got the tanks loaded with the appropriate ammunition.

The tanks were secured and began to return to the tank park. Mike told the driver, Johnny

Dole, to crank it up and they started back to the park. Johnny could really drive that tank; he made the ride as smooth as possible, like in a baby carriage. When the crew got back to the park, they had to clean the guns and the side stowage boxes on the tank, also called sponson boxes,

were opened and the cleaning staff for the 90mm gun was removed. This staff is a series

of aluminum rods about 4 feet long that are screwed together. A steel brush was attached

and cleaning fluid was applied and the staff was run repeatedly in and out of the guntube.

At the same time, the loader was cleaning the 30-caliber machine gun. When this was done

Mike took apart the 50-caliber machine gun, teaching the others how and telling them how to set

headspace on the guns. Most weapons have headspace, some are preset, but on machine –guns,

the 30 is done with the barrel screwed all the way in, then backed off a certain number of clicks. On the 50, a head space and timing gauge are used, this is a machined, precision piece

That caliber helps apply the needed headspace on the gun.

After cleaning the guns, the inside of the turret was cleaned, as was the outside, this was

done with a firehouse and the tank was left to dry and covered with the tarp.

CHAPTER THREE

In 1965, the battalion got the word to load for Vietnam and the dragon was loaded, its equipment bought up to date. It was loaded on a train flatcar and trucked to San Diego

where it was loaded on an Icu, which is a landing craft utility and can carry two tanks.

It was taken to an LSD, which is a landing ship dock, which carries cargo. The rear of the ship is lowered and water flooded in so the smaller boats can float in. The tanks are then unloaded

and driven to certain positions on the floor of the ship, then they are tied down with turn

buckles, four to each tank, then the crew takes its equipment off and goes to their quarters.

Work is still done on the Dragon to get it ready for whatever is going to happen. The Dragon

sat on the deck while the crew cleaned it up and tried keeping the delicate sights and other stuff clear of salt from the ocean. When they weren't working on the tank, the crew was doing

calisthenics and attending classes on such things as how to make range cards, which are

cards made of scrap cardboard and are used for night firing, and how to make use on the azimuth indicator and m13 elevation quadrant. Both instruments use mills to get azimuth and elevation

and range. These range cards are made up in daytime and are made to indicate targets the tank will engage at night.

Map reading was also taught along with refresher courses on the machine guns and how to

headspace and time the 50-caliber machine gun. Classes on first aid are also taught. There are arguments between the sailors and marines over things like taking showers. Fresh water is scarce and to take a shower aboard ship, you wet down, soap up, wash, rinse off, and then you're done. There are also times when nothing is done, just lay around and relax. There are moments when groups of sailors and marines get together to play poker or sing.

Sometimes the chow (food) onboard ship is good and at times it isn't. The dragon is clean and places painted.

The fording kit is repaired.

The fording kit is a kit used to help the tank ford a river or go abroad ship. The kit contains

an exhaust stack that sends the exhaust over the turret and keeps the water out. It also contains waterproof tape and a type of gunk that is used to waterproof the lights and block ports. With this kit, the

tank can ford a river 12 to 14 feet deep; the stack is taken off to work around it.

CHAPTER FOUR

In about two weeks, the ships stop at Okinawa, home of the third marine division, of which the crew and the company now become part. Here, they will pick up the pace of their training, engage in more live fire of all the guns, and, something new, jungle training. This takes place in

the northern training area of Okinawa. This area is jungle type of terrain. This means patrolling in the jungle, learning how to survive in it, how to fight in it, and how to camouflage the tank using natural foliage.

The crew learned how to live off the land and fight in it. There are field problems, or exercises. The crew camouflaged the Dragon so good one time that the platoon leader walked into the tank, hitting his head on the guntube.

"That is a good cammo job, Sergeant," the lieutenant said and

he stayed around to ask questions, which the crew answered, then he left. The crew got the word to move and they drove off with a small tree in the cargo rack on the turret.

The cargo rack is where the crew keeps their gear and any spare ammo or anything else.

On the turret, alongside the cargo rack, is a rack for the water can and oilcan. Most tanks had

an extension welded to the can racks to extend them so two cans could be placed there instead of one. The tank moved to the company area where the company would stay for the night.

The crew went over the tank doing what maintenance was required and then they laid out their shelter. Since it was hot and not the rainy season, the only thing really needed was mosquito netting.

A few weeks later the company mounted out (loaded up all their gear) and went to Vietnam.

After a week abroad ship, we landed at Chulai. This was 1965, the company set up camp in hardback tents, which are nothing more than frames of wood built about shoulder high, and a general-purpose tent pulled over that. All the company did was support the different battalions of infantry.

One of the platoons was sent to support the army, the other two platoons and the two headquarters tanks were sent to what ever mission there was. The Dragon's platoon was split, and the Dragon and its mate went to support the India company of the 7th marines on a hill about five miles away.

He reported to the commanding officer. Sergeant Johnson was given a place to put his two tanks and told the commander he would put the tanks in place within that place. The place was about one hundred yards from the hill. The men set up a pretty good shelter and built a shower unit; it was made from two 55 gallon oil drums one placed on top of the frame, the other along side and a pump to get the water from one to the other. At night, the tanks were to go to the hill and watch for infiltrators. With the help of its infrared light and scopes, it could see in the dark. During the first week, nothing happened. Then, on a Monday night, lights were seen moving just beyond a hedgerow that also contained bamboo. Sergeant Johnson took his infrared binoculars and watched as the V.C. came closer

to the Dragon. The big 90mm barked once, then again, then fell silent. There was a soft click, then the 30-caliber machine gun went off. Red tracers laced the night and bounced off rocks and chewed up the bodies of those left.

A few hours before, Sergeant Johnson and Corporal Norman made out a range card and Mike had the loader load a canister in the chamber of the 90mm and set the safety. When the attack came, the range card was thrown out because they didn't come from the direction everyone thought they would and Sergeant Johnson, who was in the turret, yelled "fire". The loader took off the 90mm safety and the gunner pulled the trigger. The loader loaded another canister and the gunner fired again, then he flicked on the infrared light and shot up the enemy that had survived the canister, which weren't many. The white light came on and the whole line opened up. Then, when the light went off, the line ceased fire. During the small amount of time the light was on, they could see the bodies of the dead V.C.; they were cut down like cordwood. The 1281 .38 caliber pellets in the canister had done the job.

The next day the Dragon was again on the hill and Sergeant Johnson was getting into the turret when a bullet whined past his ear and another ricocheted off the cupola. He went to the range finder and was looking for the sniper and it took him half an hour before he spotted him. He moved to the 50 caliber sight and looked for about twenty minutes before the man moved and he fired a twenty round burst at the place where the sniper was then followed with another twenty round burst. The infantry went out and found the sniper shot full of holes; he looked like a sieve.

The infantry Sergeant gave the sniper's rifle to Mike and he put it in the turret. The next day they got the word to join the rest of the platoon at another hill. They took down the shelter and shower. The shower was loaded on the engine cover and they joined the rest of the platoon a few miles south. The reason for the move was North

Vietnam expected an attack and they needed the
    extra firepower.

When they got there, the platoon sergeant asked, "What the hell you got on the back?"

When Mike told him, a big grin came over his unshaven face and he told Mike where to put the Dragon, and the shower was put up nearby.

The attack came, but the South Vietnamese took the brunt of it and stopped it in three days. The platoon packed up and left for the command post. On the way, the platoon had to bypass a bridge. The water wasn't deep, but the mud was bad, it had been turned up by the passage on many vehicles. When the third tank went through, it got stuck. That meant it had to be towed out by the others.

One tank was hooked up, but couldn't move it, so all four tanks had to be hooked up. This is done by using the tow cables that are carried on each tank. There are four towing shackles to which the cables are attached. They are crossed and in an emergency, as the final drive is not disconnected, this was successful in getting the stuck tank out and the platoon proceeded to the rear.

Upon arrival, Mike was told his tank was due for a hundred hour check, which means the engine had to be removed. That afternoon, the crew set about getting the Dragon ready to have its engine removed. The engine cover was loosened by using the big socket wrench, then the maintenance crew, with help of the retriever, lifts the cover off the vehicle; then all the wiring is disconnected, along with the final drive, which is the gear that connects the drive sprocket and final drive to the transmission. This is done by loosening a simple bolt and unclasping a brass ring, then moving a gear assembly. The aluminum transmission cover is removed and the engine mounts loosened and the retriever moves in with the engine sling and lifts it up and out of the vehicle and sets it on a platform to be worked on.

CHAPTER FIVE

The crew climbs into the engine compartment and begins the job of cleaning it out. One of the crew goes under the tank and removes all the inspection plates, which are bolted to the bottom of the vehicle. This insures that the water used to clean it will drain properly. While cleaning wrenches, pens and cigarette lighters are found under the gunk. The torsion bars, which are made of tungsten carbide steel and determine how rough the ride will be for the crew, are inspected to insure that they are not broken. The maintenance crew works on the engine and in a few days, it's replaced and the Dragon is again on the move. This time it's beach guard. At night, Viet Cong had hit the airstrip at Da Nang and Chu Lai. They had come in from the beach in small boats. The tanks, with their searchlights, can pick out any intruders before they can get onto the beach.

The crew takes the Dragon down to the beach and it is positioned in the area where the sand meets the trees. It is set in so it is not in the same spot each time it goes to the beach.

On the third night, Corporal Norman is on watch when he spots something out on the water. He wakes up the sergeant, who then takes over. They illuminate the object and it is a small boat and they are told to sink it, but Mike sees that it is a just a family passing and radios the fact to the rear. He keeps an eye on it. However, an hour later a small boat was sighted and it was a boatload of enemy soldiers and Mike was ordered to sink it. Both machine guns were bought to bear on it and it was sunk, then the men in the water were taken under fire. In the early light of morning, the bodies of the dead soldiers had floated ashore and they had to be taken care of: buried. The Dragon

was returned to the rear and immediately the air cleaners were taken care of as the vehicle's performance was bad.

Corporal Dole opened the air cleaners by using a small socket to remove a small bole, then the frame was removed and the cloth bags were removed and beaten against the tank and

replaced. In the next few days, the beach guard goes on until the platoon is assigned to support an infantry battalion in an operation. The Dragon was fully loaded with a full complement of ammo and the platoon took off. After a few miles it was ambushed, but due to the training in road march security, it wasn't caught off guard. A yell over the radio and the sound of machine gun fire and the flaming tail of an antitank rocket alerted the crew who immediately returned fire.

Mike immediately bought the turret to bear on the direction from which the fire was coming from and immediately opened fire with the 30 caliber, followed by the 50 caliber, then a few rounds of canister and the ambush was broken. The sound of the rounds hitting the turret was like hail on a tin roof with all five tanks firing and only one hit with RPG. The platoon moved to a secure area where the wounded were taken care of. When replacements were gotten, the platoon moved on to its assignment where the tanks were used improperly by the infantry, they wouldn't use them as support. It was corrected by the platoon , sergeant and the operation was a success and the Dragon returned to the rear.

CHAPTER SIX

The time had come for the crew to go home; its time in the country was up. A new crew was assigned to the Dragon. The whole 1st division had arrived a year to the day of the Dragon's landing. The new crew was young and mostly inexperienced. There was a big operation coming up and the crew was getting the Dragon ready to go. A full load of fuel and ammo was aboard and they moved out and linked up with the infantry and were being used as a blocking force

for the operation. The attack had begun and there was a unit in the vacinity of the Dragon.

They were hit by at least a company and a rocket propelled grenade hit the Dragon and

the gunner and commander were killed. The inside of the turret went from white to pink with the spattering of blood and body parts.

The loader was wounded, as was the driver. After the operation, the tank was cleaned up repaired and a new crew is assigned to the Dragon. The hole that was made by the RPG was repaired by pushing a steel rod through the hole and cutting it off on both ends. But, this seemed to affect the Dragon, it didn't operate the way it did with the original crew. The engine didn't catch

at the first try to start it like it did with the original crew. The sights fogged up and a couple of times the electral system went out. It spent a lot of time in the maintenance shop. Finally one day

everything worked fine and just in time for a new operation: road security escorting columns of vehicles down the road. At first nothing happened, but on the third day of the third week

the Dragon hit a mine. It was a 500-pound bomb and it blew the track off and two sets of road wheels cracked the hull just under the drivers compartment. The explosion also killed the driver, blowing him up against the closed position. It broke his back, literally, crushed his skull,

and also blew his insides all over the compartment. It also killed the loader as blew the gunner's legs off just below the knees. The Dragon was blown over on its side. The commander was blown free of the tank because he was standing in his hatch. Later that day, a retriever, which is like a wrecker truck, but is on a tank hull designed to pull the tank and anything else, righted the tank and pulled it back to the rear area where it was inspected. It was determined that

it was not fit for combat and was to be used for spare parts. So, after the blood and guts were cleaned out, it was stripped of all useable equipment and was hauled into a field to be used as a target.

So the dragon's bite has been removed, its original crew scattered to the far ends of the earth

and the only evidence it ever existed is in pictures and the memory of the crew. Now only

those parts removed from it are able to carry on the dragon's odyssey.

THE END`

The Transparent Detective

A fantasy by Art Allen

Arthur Allen

It was 1967 and he had been in Vietnam for three years: all but 1 year spent in prison camps. This

was his third escape. As he sat and thought back, it rapidly came to him.

It was in 1964, he had been a commander on a tank that was guarding a bridge. It was in the

last month of his first tour in country and was looking forward to going home, but the Viet Cong

had other ideas. They hit the bridge at about 4:30 and it was bad. The first thing was a sound, it

alerted the crew and the rocket propelled grenade hit the front of the tank and bounced up and hit

the gun.

The driver had gotten into his compartment, but hadn't yet closed his hatch when the rocket hit and he was killed outright. The blast had disabled the gun and the machine guns were bought to bear and

another rocket hit the tank on the left of the turret and killed the loader. Some of the hot metal killed the gunner and wounded him. The other tank was also hit, but not as bad. He broke open the first aid kit and applied a pressure bandage to his thigh wound and his arm. He looked at the remains of his crew and cussed the higher command because they hadn't told the truth about the area he was in. It was supposed to be cleared and a convoy was supposed to come through, but it had been cancelled and he hadn't been

told and the enemy had come into the area.

He began to engage the enemy with his .50 caliber machine gun and took as many of them as he

could when the gun ran out of ammo. He took his submachine gun and some grenades. He placed

a thermite grenade in the breach of the 90mm gun and closed it. The grenade would fuse the breach shut.

He checked the load in his pistol and opened his hatch and looked out. He shot a V.C. off the tank and hopped out, spraying the area with .45 ammo and jumped down off the tank. The shock of his wound halted him for just second. He looked around and caught a couple of them as they ran toward him. The burst caught them and halted them in place and lifted them. It was as if a giant hand slapped them back.

A grenade took care of the rest.

That took care of them for a while and he climbed back on the tank to get the identity tags from his dead crew. He also took the extra ammo magazines; he was going to need them. He looked for the other tank and saw it moving. He tried to run to it and waved. It stopped and the commander yelled for him to haul ass.

He limped toward it and a burst of gunfire cut the ground in front of him, but he didn't stop. He ran toward the tank and when he was close, he threw the id tags at the commander and yelled at him to get the hell out of there. Then, he turned and fired a burst of fire at the enemy and headed toward the jungle as the tank pulled away.

As he came to the jungle, he was hit by a rifle butt and knocked out. When he came around, he was bound. His wrists were tied behind him, a piece of bamboo was thrust through the space where his arm bent and behind his back. The V.C. pulled on it to cause pain and they kicked and hit him, yelling at him in their language. A rope was placed around his neck and he was pulled forward. He tried to resist and was kicked. He tried to kick back and was clubbed down to the ground. Blood poured from his mouth as he was pulled to his feet and led into the jungle. They came to a camp and he was tied to a tree until a pit was dug and a cage built. It was made of bamboo, square, and was put in the hole. He was pulled to his feet, the bamboo stick pulled from behind his back, his wrists were untied, and he was thrown into the cage.

He escaped a few days later when they tried to take him to be questioned. He ran into the jungle and in a week, he was recaptured and again thrown into to cage. He escaped twice more. Each time he did, he was closer to North Vietnam. This time, the third, he figured he was about five miles inside North Vietnam.

He had taken refuge in a cave and had survived for two weeks on snakes and bugs. He had taken a knife from a guard when he knocked him out. He didn't take a rifle because he didn't want a firefight with them

and risk being killed now, so he only took the knife and a compass and matches. He headed south and found this cave on the seventh day. He knew that the Cong knew about this cave and he would be moving.

He left the cave and was about a mile away when they caught him. He wasn't watching the trail and tripped over a wire and they jumped on him. It took six of them to get his six-foot frame into ropes again.

He was again taken to a camp, only this time a Major told him, "You will be here only a short time; you

will be moved further north under heavy guard."

He was put in a cage and kept there until it was time for him to be taken north. It was about three days and he was herded into a truck and four guards were on board as the truck moved out.

They were on the road a long time. There were stops where he was tied to trees and fed a little. One of the guards was awake at all times. The truck came to a border; it was the border between Vietnam and China. He

was pulled off the truck and was pushed toward the gate. It was lifted and he was pushed across.

An officer there told him, "You have escaped too many times. Here, you will not escape. It will be your death if you try."

He was put in another truck and it took off. He was only allowed off the truck to relieve himself. On the trip he slept as much as he could, it seemed like forever, but it was about a week.

The truck pulled into a camp and he was pulled down. The camp was big. It was walled in. The wall was about ten feet high, the gate was steel. He was led to a cell and the bindings taken off. He was pushed into the cell. He stopped and looked around, saying out loud, "Well, Mike, you're in for it now. You'll never get out."

A voice said, "Don't believe that." Mike turned to see an old man. He was crouched in a corner. He was in a cut off smock that had once been white. His hair was long and he had a fumanchu mustache and beard.

"You are an American?"

Mike said, "Yeah, I'm an American," and he sat down on the floor holding his pants up as he had lost weight and had to hold them up.

CHAPTER TWO

The old man told Mike who he was, "My name is Chang. I was a chemist and doctor, but I do not

agree with the government, so I was imprisoned and moved around until I came here. I am the camp doctor and have access to the laboratory and I can do my experiments as I see fit, as long as I do not

try to escape."

The next morning he was fed some kind of soup. It smelled awful, but he ate it and was told he would work in the mine. It was a uranium mine and he was sure it was the end for him.

The day was long, about ten hours, and when he went back to the cell, Chang was gone, but he returned

later in the day. He had a rat in his pocket and said, "This is Min, he is my subject I am trying to make him

invisible."

Mike laughed.

But, Chang smiled and said, "That is typical, but I think I can do it. I just have to find the right chemicals and combination of them and that is where Min comes in. He is my guinea pig, so to speak."

Mike lay on his pallet and they talked about their lives. Chang was born in Nanking in the early

nineteen hundreds and was put in prison when the commies came to power. That was after World War II, and he had been in prison ever since. They kept him alive because he was a doctor and chemist. He had been working on this invisibility for along time and felt he was close.

Mike told him of his childhood in Connecticut, of fishing as a kid, and baseball and football, then

his family's move to California, and his enlistment in the Marines and how he was captured. Chang

smiled and asked, "Did you kill a lot of them?"

Mike said, "As many as I could." Then he fell asleep. He worked as hard as he could and Chang kept at his work. One day Mike came back to the cell and Chang was smiling.

Mike asked, "What are you so happy about?" He hopped up, "Michael, it worked. Min is here, but he is invisible. Look." He pointed at the straw on the floor and it was moving. At a bare spot it stopped and began on the other side. He had done it. Chang took a watch from his pocket. "I want to see how long he stays that way." I sat on my pallet and fell asleep. In a while, Chang woke me up. "Mike, he was invisible for an hour. Now, all I have to do is figure out how much he weighs and apply that to something bigger to see how much of the serum to use."

He took a pad from its hiding place and a pencil and began to figure as Mike went back to sleep.

Mike was up the next morning and Chang was gone to the sick room as he went off to the mine. When

he returned that night,

Chang said, "Mike, I have figured out the weight ratio and I want to use you on this. Maybe we can help you escape in this way."

"Okay," Mike said.

Chang took a needle from his pocket and swabbed a part of Mike's arm and injected some of the serum into him. In a few minutes, Chang gasped and held a piece of a mirror up to show Mike that it was working. Mike didn't see anything in the mirror and he put a hand to his face and could feel something, but couldn't see the hands.

Chang said, "Lay on your pallet. I'll stay up and time it." So mike lay down and went to sleep.

He woke to a commotion and could see men in the cell looking under the straw and Chang had a little smile on his face. Mike knew he was not seen and he moved around the cell, avoiding the men so they couldn't touch him. When they left, he did too and went to the mine. In a few hours he came out and the guards ran to him, clubbing him and the commander of the camp demanded to know where he was. Mike told him, "I'm sorry, sir. I was so tired, I fell asleep in the mine way back in a corner in the shadows."

The commander bought it and told him to go back to his cell. When he got there, he told Chang that he was in the mine until almost daylight. And Chang figured it was

72 hours. Mike went to sleep. He woke in eight hours and Chang told him, "It lasted for 72 hours and eight hours of uninterrupted sleep will replenish you.

Now all I have to do is find some way to administer it." He went to his lab as Mike went to the mine.

CHAPTER THREE

For four days, Mike didn't see Chang and on the fifth night, after he returned to the cell, Chang told

him, "Michael, I did I found a way to administer it: this ring. I put some of the serum in it and attached a needle with a hollow point. All you have to do is turn it and you're gone. I know. I tried. It works." He handed Mike the ring and it fit his pinkie finger.

He took it off and hid it in his pallet with some things he had been collecting and said, "Chang, you have worked hard. Rest and take it easy, you are no longer a young man."

Chang said, "I am tired. I think I'll go to bed." And they both went to sleep.

The next day after Mike returned to the cell, he was unhappy to see that Chang had been beaten

badly. He went to him and asked, "Chang, what happened?"

"They found Min had disappeared and reappeared and told me I would make it available to them and when I refused they beat me." Sometime in the night Chang died and Mike vowed to get away. He watched all the men in the prison the guards only, and had found very tall and well-built Chinese, and knew that that was the man he would take out when it was time to go.

Two nights later, as the guards went to lock the cell, he put paper in the lock hole. That prevented the lock from locking. Then, he went to his pallet, took the ring and serum and his other stuff. He turned the ring, felt a prick, and waited. He looked in the mirror; he was invisible and he pushed on the door. It opened; he removed the paper and it locked. He moved in the shadows to the place the tall man was. He looped a rope around the man's neck and choked him to death, then he took the man's clothes and turned the ring in the opposite direction and he became visible and went out the gate and was gone.

Traveling invisible was fun; he could steal anything and get away with it. In 72 hours he found a place to hide and slept 8 full hours. He went invisible and went on his way again. He came to a small village

and saw a policeman beating an old man. He went to them and, as the cop raised his arm, Mike grabbed

the cop's arm and held it as the man struggled to get away. The look in his eyes, a look of pure terror

when he couldn't see the reason his arm stopped. Mike pushed the man and he fell, he yelled, got to his feet and ran off. Mike laughed and suddenly stopped as he realized that the old man was looking at him or at the place he was. The old man crossed himself and quickly went on his way. Mike went in the direction the cop went and came to a police station. He looked in a window at the cop trying to explain what happened to him.

His superior hit him and yelled at someone. A man came in and took him away. Mike went on his way

and came to a river and saw a man pushing a small boat into the river. He went and stepped into it. He moved to the bow and sat as the man moved the boat the middle of the river and turned it south. Mike

decided to stay on until he could see where they were bound. They had been on the water for about an hour when the man turned the boat toward the opposite bank from which he had gotten aboard. When the boat hit the shore, Mike was off and gone inland.

He needed a map and stopped at a store and lifted one. As he moved out the door, someone yelled and pointed at the map as it floated out the door. As the storeowner chased it, the map seemed to pick up speed and move into an alley where Mike stopped turned the ring to appear then again to disappear.

Just as Mike and the map disappeared, the store owned appeared at the alley entrance and stopped, the map had vanished. He stared at the place. As Mike moved past him, the man seemed to feel that someone passed him. He turned to look the way Mike went and shook his head and returned to his store.

Mike went on his way and came upon a shed into which he went. He unfolded the map, found north, and

placed the map so it showed the coast. He figured he had about another fifty miles to Hong Kong and

he would have the army looking for him. But, he knew that he would not be found if he had anything to say about it. It was getting close to the time he had to rest and he found a barn with a loft and hid in the hay and fell asleep. He was startled awake by voices and slowly looked down into the barn and saw a farmer and his people. They were talking. It looked like the farmer was assigning tasks to his people, so Mike lay back and slept.

He woke in the dark and moved out and went to the nearest town, where he broke into a store to steal a watch. He had been relying on the sun to try and tell time, so he needed the watch. He took a pocket watch and

left. As he neared the edge of the town, he heard a vehicle coming and saw a truck. As it passed, he jumped on and settled down among the boxes and tried to think.

He drifted off to sleep and awoke when the truck jerked to a stop. He looked out and saw the driver go into a store to buy food. Mike went in and found

the place crowded and was able to steal food and drink, then he went back to the truck and climbed in.

The driver came out and they were on their way. He devoured the food and drank the liquid that tasted like Coke and settled back to sleep.

The truck rumbled on and he could see rice paddies and small villages and towns. The driver stopped to get food along the way. When he could, he slept and rejuvenated himself. He woke to rain beating on the top of the truck and sat upright an hey jumped and yelled they stared at the gun that seemed to float in mid air and the officer tried to grab the weapon and danced as it turned on him and fired at his feet then dropped to the ground and as Mike stepped back the men were crazy running around and screaming, The officer was standing looking at the gun laying on the ground and slowly bent down to pick it up. Mike hurried and, as the man stooped over, he kicked him in the ass. The officer grabbed the weapon and turned and shot the man standing next to where Mike was standing as he had moved.

The officer yelled and the men picked up the body and went back to their hut. The officer motioned the driver to move. Mike jumped aboard and the vehicle went on its way.

The driver stopped the truck and came around to the rear and in good English said, "Hello? Are you there? I think there is someone there."

Mike turned his ring and the man jumped and Mike told him about himself the driver began to laugh. When Mike frowned, he shook his head and explained about the officer back at the road block and then he looked Mike in the eye and said, "I will help you get out of China if you will help me to get a man who murdered my wife. He is living in Hong Kong on the money he took from me."

Mike told him he would help and got in the cab for the rest of the trip. The driver introduced himself as Quang Chi and Mike introduced himself and they continued on to Hong Kong.

After crossing the border, they asked questions and Quang found where the man he was looking for lived. They went there, but before they entered, Mike turned the ring and they proceeded to the man's room.

When they got there, the man looked at Quang and laughed, but when Mike grabbed his throat, the man

cried out and he told Quang everything. Mike moved to a window and threw him out. The man fell four stories landing on the sidewalk. Quang was on the sidewalk when the man hit, so he wasn't involved. Mike took off and when he passed Quang he said, "I'm going to the U.S. Embassy."

CHAPTER FOUR

Upon entering Hong Kong, Quang and Mike had stopped and gotten proper clothing. After doing in the man for Quang, Mike proceeded to the American Embassy. At the gate he told the police officer that

he was an American and wanted to go in. The Marine at the entrance was watching and Mike said, "Hey, Corporal, I'm an escaped POW and need in." The corporal let him in and told him to go to the office of the

CIA officer. The man in the office asked when he was a POW and when he escaped and Mike told him.

He asked if he could have some new clothes, a shower, and some fresh milk. The man said, "Yes."

The hot water cascaded over his skinny body and felt so good that he stayed there for most of an hour.

They had gotten new uniforms for him that would eventually have to be changed when he got back to his normal weight of 260 pounds. He dressed and the Marine with him took him to the mess hall to eat. The cook asked him what he wanted.

"A nice, juicy, well-done steak and a baked potato, and some veggies, and some fruit if you have any, and some cold milk." They set a carton of milk in front of him and a big glass. He filled the glass and slowly drank it, then filled it again and drank that one.

They bought the steak and he slowly ate it, savoring each bite as if he had never had one before.

He had put steak sauce on it and he licked his lips as he ate each piece, then attacked the fruit. He then went back to the interaction room and there they had his records, it had been sent by diplomatic pouch.

The officer said, "Well, you are who you say you are. Let's continue."

He told them all of it even, the part where he could become invisible and proved it by turning the ring. He said, "Don't try to take the ring and duplicate it; only works with my DNA and no one else can copy it."

They put him up in a room and he hung out with the Marines there. They talked about his imprisonment

and his escapes and they took him on liberty in the city and they got drunk. Mike felt like a Marine again.

In three days the C.I.A station chief told Mike he had gotten in touch with his superiors in Washington and

he wanted Mike to go to work for them. Mike asked, "Can I think about it for a few days?" The chief okayed it

and Mike went to his room to think. In two days he contacted the man and said, "Okay, if the company will open an account and place one million dollars a year in it." Then he told the Chief that he had worked in an uranium mine and had been exposed to radiation and that the combination of the radiation and serum

made him invisible and that for some strange reason, anything he has on him at the time of the change also

becomes invisible. He didn't know how or why, but that's it; if he was holding a camera with film in it

they also became invisible.

The station chief had again been in touch with Washington and he came to Mike and said, "You

will go home first on leave, then go to Washington for some classes." Mike was given an airline ticket home. He reported to CIA Head quarters after he came off leave and began another debriefing where he told of his escape and how the serum worked in his system; he could control how long he could stay invisible up to 72 hours, and he needed 8 hours of rest to replenish himself. He got an apartment not

far from the place he would be learning some things he would need to survive and some of the

Russian, Korean and Arabic languages.

In the apartment, he furnished it to his liking and bought a comfortable bed: he vowed he would sleep comfortable. He started classes the next day and found it boring, but he learned them. He also found it fun to scare people by being invisible and moving things as they watched. He was in a 7-11 and and out of sight of the people and turned his ring and went invisible and took a bottle of Coke to the counter. The clerk screamed and ran out. Mike paid for the drink and left, the bottle floating in air. People moved as he went along the street. He went into a restroom and switched back to normal and left, going back to class

where he resumed the learning of languages or enough to get by.

There was an oil shortage in the country, or every one thought so, and the FBI asked the CIA to lend Mike to them and they did. He went into a shed and came out, but no one saw him. He was let out of a cab and the driver was staring at the open door and he sped away so fast that the cops pulled him over. Mike grinned and whispered good luck to the man and went inside to the office of the C.E.O. and waited until night when he went through the files and got proof that the oil companies were in fact price gouging. He took out his camera out and copied all the papers and put them back and left. He called the FBI and told them

He had the information and where to meet him.

The F.B.I. came to the public park and Mike was leaning against a tree. He had a camera hanging around his neck and his hands were in his pockets. The two men who were to meet him were careful coming toward him and they had their hands in their pockets. Mike took his hands out of his pockets and held his left hand in his right to turn the ring if it was necessary. One of the men said, "Mike Wilson?" And Mike nodded.

They identified themselves and escorted him to a car that went to headquarters where he turned over the film to the headman.

He left and went to his place. He entered and was immediately grabbed from behind and another man hit him, knocking him out. When he came to, he was tied to a chair and a man was very mad. He had Mike's ring and was yelling, "The ring does not work."

Mike laughed and told the guy, "It only works with my DNA you idiot," and he was hit again. The man mistakenly threw the thing at him and Mike put it on his finger and turned it as the men reached for him.

He disappeared and they jumped back and looked around. As they did, he got loose from the rope and proceeded toward them.

He picked up a piece of wood and as one turned he was hit in the face. Another was coming from behind when Mike thrust the wood to the rear hitting this guy in the sternum and then giving him a vertical stroke that broke his jaw. The leader pulled a gun and Mike dropped the wood so the man couldn't hit him. He stepped to his right and, as the man fired, he grabbed his arm, pulled him forward, and slammed an elbow into his face breaking his nose. Then he turned the gun into the man's stomach and pulled the trigger twice.

The muffled shots and the scream from the man fell on only Mike's ears.

Mike went through their pockets and took their IDs and called the department and told them to come get him and them; he would wait. He waited and the men started to come around. Two went to the third and saw that he was dead, then realized that their IDs were gone and that Mike was gone. They tried to leave and heard his voice, "No you don't. You're staying here," and felt something grab their arms. The guy

with the broken jaw was slapped and yelled as he put a hand to it. They both stopped and, as the FBI

men came up, they put their hands up. Mike appeared and the men jumped, "Don't do that," He turned them over to the men. He went back with them and wanted to know how they found out about him.

Mike was suspicious of these people and decided to spy on the man. That night he went as if to leave and instead he went into a rest room and came out invisible and went to the office he had come from. He waited and when he saw one of the men that had come to meet him the other day, he followed him into the office and stood in the corner. As they talked, he took a recorder from his pocket and taped everything that was said between the three men in the room. All three were in on the conspiracy to get information to the enemies of the country. When they left, so did he and he went to the director and played the tape.

He was in the room when they took the men into custody. He smiled at them as they passed and said, "You really should have used your head. You must have known I would get onto you sooner or later."

The head man growled, "I thought it would have been later and not so soon."

They were tried and sentenced to

life in prison. Mike was assigned to Russia, but only to spy on them and get any information he could.

He went to the office of one of the high military officers, invisible, and photographed all the papers on his desk and in his safe.

In six months, he photographed thousands of items and taped hours of information, all while acting as a tourist. All thought he had the secret police stymied as to what he was up to. They searched Mike's room and found nothing because he left it all invisible. They found nothing and found nothing at the airport when he left the country. When he got back to the States and the film was developed, they found that the Russians had no intention of living up to a treaty that had been made and also tapes of them and new weapons they were testing.

Mike was next assigned to London; he had always wanted to go there and now he was. He checked in with the head of Scotland Yard, the equivalent of the FBI, and MI-5, the equivalent of the CIA. They got him a flat, as they called an apartment, nearby and an expense account. He helped them solve crimes they couldn't and on his free time he went to the military museum and to the national museum He went to Ireland to help capture members of the IRA that were still at large and did it by infiltrating the organization. Of course, it was all done by his ability to become invisible.

CHAPTER FIVE

He spent about six months in England. Not only did he help Scotland Yard and MI-5, he also found out

what the English were doing to the United States in the way of Intelligence, which really wasn't much.

Mike liked the people and made friends. The British had tried to get the secret of his invisibility, but he told

them as he told the Russians that it was his DNA along with the serum that did it.

He got a call from the agency sending him to Israel, where he worked with the Mosad, the Israeli

Equivalent to the C.I.A. While there, he helped take down some big wheels in the Hamas. In one

deal, he was in Lebanon and was in a room with some Arabs and decided to have some fun. They

were sitting around playing cards, their weapons laying around, so he being in his invisible mode, picked up a pistol and moved. One of the men saw the weapon move and yelled. Pointing and yelling, he jumped up and the weapon pointed at him and fired. The round hit the wall beside his ear and he was out the window in an instant. The weapon then pointed at another and he went out the window. Another grabbed his rifle and fired one round; it grazed Mike and Mike put two bullets in the man's head, then he dropped it and went out and to his room. Once there, he became visible and tended to his wound, which wasn't bad; it just pissed him off. It grazed the top of his right shoulder, breaking the skin. He opened his first aid kit and applied some salve and a bandage.

He next went to Libya, where he got the locations of all the terrorist camps. In doing so, he had proof

that the Libyans were, in fact, hiding them in the desert. He then went to Syria to prove the same thing.

In fact, he went to all the Arab countries to prove that they were supporting terrorists. This would help the United Nations in proving to the world this was happening and sanctions could be bought to bear on them. He toured Egypt as a tourist and agent getting intelligence along the way.

All this intelligence was sent back to the agency by diplomatic pouch. All his films and audiotapes

were sent along with documents he stole. While in Egypt, he went along on a tour of the Valley of the Kings

and was amazed as was everyone else at the size of the pyramids and the tour of the museums that

held the artifacts from the tombs.

He was called home to work for the FBI, going after local militia groups and skinheads that were causing so much trouble. Then he was asked to work on the mob. He helped in bringing down the most dangerous members by sitting in on their meetings, deals, and the killings and knew where the bodies were

buried, literally. He spent a total of four years working for these people and was very suspicious, so he got inside information to protect himself against them. This information could send people to prison if it ever got out. So, at the end of his tenure with them, he said he wanted out and when they hesitated, he told them of the information he had and that it was out of their reach and only he could get at it. First, he wanted confirmation that all the countries he had worked for had, in fact, had deposited the money he asked for. If they hadn't he would release information on them that was secret to them alone and would put them in jail.

A check was made and all the money was there. There was a total of five million dollars, so they terminated his contract with the proviso that if he was needed in the future they could call.

CHAPTER SIX

He informed them that he would become a private detective. They issued him a license that

was good nationwide. He was also issued a permit to carry concealed weapons.

He moved to California in the San Diego area, to be exact. There he bought a warehouse that

was a two-story building that was near the ocean. In fact, the rear of the building was on the water.

He contracted to have the place done over like he wanted it. On the first floor, in front, he had them put in a garage to hold a Camaro convertible and a Hummer, which is a civilian copy of a military vehicle

and wider than most cars. Also in that area was a stairway leading up to the second floor. On the other side of the wall of the garage he had a small gym installed with all the latest workout gear. Also in that area he had a place to work on his hobby, which was building models, both aircraft and armored vehicles, and glass showcases to put them in.

The upper level consisted of his office area and living quarters. His kitchen was the most modern

he could get. He was in the area of the local pound when he decided to stop in and he found a pair

of Rottweiler puppies that had been abandoned. He bought them and went to a pet store and bought all the things they would need. It took about three weeks to get the building in the order he wanted. All the inside

stuff was done and he wanted the outside done in the following manner: the side was torn up and a lawn was planted along with a few trees, and on the waterside a small pier was put in. He went to a local boat dealer and bought a small yacht, about a twenty-footer, that he had fully stocked. When the dock was ready, the boat was tied to it.

He was sitting in his living room playing with the dogs when his phone rang. It was a potential client and he told the person to come to his place tomorrow at ten in the morning. Mike was in his hobby room

working on a model after a strenuous workout in his gym when the dogs began acting up, which usually meant someone was near. The old ship's bell clanged twice. He had put a sign up stating to ring twice every few seconds until the door was answered. He went through the gym to the main door, which was between

the garage and gym. A short hall access to the door was along the old loading dock. Mike had a set of

Stairs built into it with a small roof to protect people from the weather. He opened the door. A woman of about thirty was standing looking at the place. She was dressed casually in clean jeans and a plaid blouse. Her hair was brown and hung to her shoulders. She was average looking; a young mom with a problem.

" Come in," he said and opened the door to the stairs. The dogs had gone through the doggie door and up the stairs.

She sat in a chair at his motion and as he asked, "How can I help you," she said "i

was told about you by Lieutenant Bob Franks of the police. He said you would help me." Her son had lost his dad in an accident in the Navy

and he was hanging out a bunch of kids. One of them had slapped her when she tried to get her son away

and threatened to hurt her bad.

Mike asked when was the next time the boys would be coming to her place.

"Tomorrow," she smiled.

He told her he would be there tomorrow at nine a.m. and to tell them her husband's ghost was there to protect them and to leave the rest to him. He was at her place at nine and told her what he was going do. At about noon

they came. There were six of them and she again told them to leave. The leader grabbed the front of her

blouse and raised his hand. As he growled, "Told you, Bitch. Huh?" something grabbed his raised hand in a vice grip twisted and bent it back until it snapped.

The punk screamed and raised his other hand; it was also broken. He cried jumped up and yelled, "What the hell?"

Ruth told him, "That's my husband's ghost you punk.

Now get the hell out of here."

At about the same time, another punk was grabbed by the seat of his pants

and his collar and thrown out the door. Mike was almost trampled by the rest. Ruth grabbed her son,

who was all doped up, and she called 911. He had passed out. Mike started C.P.R. until the ambulance came and the kid was taken to the hospital. Mike called Franks and told him what happened and about the punk whose hands he had broken and that he would be available to identify the jerk.

Bob came by and he and Mike talked about the case. Ruth's boy had died of a drug overdose and they

had caught the punks. They were so scared that they had talked.

Bob asked, "What the hell did you do to them?"

Mike told him about himself and how he had used it to scare the kids. Bob was worried that it would taint the case. Mike explained that he had testified for the F.B.I. against the mob and that it would stand up.

Bob was interested in the fact that Mike could go invisible at anytime and he asked all kinds of questions.

One was if he would work with the police from time to time. Mike agreed and then Bob left to go back to work.

CHAPTER SEVEN

Mike got a call from the government that Mr. Chang, who had helped him escape form China, was

asking for asylum. Mike got in contact with his friends in the government and Chang and his family was granted asylum. They were flown into San Diego and Mike met them. He took Mr. Chang in his arms and hugged him and saw how much he had aged. He made arrangements to house the family until he could get his plan into effect.

Mike had thought about making his warehouse a three-story building. In all the time he was working for the government, he had invested his money and had made a fortune so he could afford it. He

Talked with the Changs and, in their grateful way, they offered to work for him. He told them of his plan and

that they were to move into the upper floor when it was done. Chang agreed and asked if his son could be his houseboy. Mike agreed if he would stay in a couple of rooms in the floor putting in. He had him tell the contractor what he wanted in the rooms and it was done. It took about six months to build the rooms on the third floor. In the mean time, he arranged for lodging for his family. He took Chang

fishing in his boat. They went out and Mike told him all about the experiences in the Chinese prison camp. He

told Mike that he had checked on the professor and they had killed him, holding him responsible for his escape. They spent the entire day talking and getting to know each other. He told Mike he had saved his life by getting the embassy to help him and eventually his family and for that he would be forever grateful.

Mike paid for his sons' education and his grandkids. They lived in his building and took care of him and the dogs and the place. They had planted grass and trees in the place where the cement was taken up and in a year a beautiful lawn was growing. They also took over care of Mike's vehicles and boat, even learning the waters around San Diego. When Mike went fishing, the boat was fully stocked with food and drink.

In the mean time, he also had a number of cases. One was of a small boy who had his dog stolen and it took him a while to find it. Mike ended up following the guy to a house in the country and had called the police when he got there. His payment was the look on the boy's face when he saw his best friend and

took him in his arms. The dog's name was Todd and it was a shepherd and was friendly to the boy and very protective. Mike had refused a divorce case where he would have to peek in windows.

CHAPTER EIGHT

Mike was sitting in his study when his houseboy, Ho My, came in and said, "Sir, there is someone here to see you. I think it is a client."

Mike said, "Okay, Ho, show the person in." The person was Franks, the police lieutenant and he wanted Mike to help in a drug case. All he wanted Mike to do was eavesdrop on the people. Mike

agreed and told Franks he would have to get his gear together and then he would go to the address

Franks gave him. Franks left.

Mike got his video camera and his tape recorder and told Ho My to let the others know he would be gone a while and took off. He arrived at the place and was in time to see a deal going down. He watched and followed the dealer to his place and went inside. The place was a mess. He hadn't cleaned it in a long time and Mike saw why; the guy didn't stay long, just long enough to make a phone call then he was gone. With Mike on his tail, the dealer got in his can and Mike climbed in the back and they took off. They crossed the border and into Tijuana to a house and there the dealer picked up a load of stuff. He had a van and

there were false panels in the van which were removed and coke was stowed there and the panels

were replaced.

Mike taped all of this, including the boss of the drug ring along with the payoff of an American

who was to ride back with the dealer. Mike got in the back and the other guy got in the passenger seat and they returned to the border where the border guard was paid off. Then they

proceeded to a warehouse in the dock area. There they met more people and the van pulled into the warehouse and it was unloaded and more money changed hands. This was all gotten on tape. Mike left and went home. In the morning he called Franks to come to his place and watch the tape.

Franks swore as he watched the tape. When asked what was wrong, Franks said, "Two of those guys are cops and they are taking payoffs."

In three days there was a raid and all the people were arrested

and the police were taken into custody. They were locked up in the same prison as some of the

people that they had locked up.

Mike went into semi-retirement. He took on some cases, some local and some not. There was the case he took that sent him to Japan where he had a part in taking down a couple of Yakuza people, the

Japanese mob. Another case took him to New York, where he spent three days following a killer

and taping his crimes: it led to his conviction and execution.

CHAPTER NINE

Mike went into total retirement and he and Chang loaded up the boat and went fishing. They stayed

Out for four days and caught a lot of fish. When they got back, they kept some fish and Chang took some to the Vietnamese people in town and was back in about an hour. That was when he fell to the floor clutching his chest. Mike called 911 and they took him to the hospital. The doctor told the nurse that he wasn't going to admit a gook that most likely didn't have any insurance. Mike went to him, grabbed him by the collar, lifted him off the floor, and told him, "This man is a better man than you ever will be and he is not a gook. He is Chinese and he saved my life. He doesn't need any insurance. I'll pay for anything he needs and I'm going to report you to the chief of this hospital." He then dropped the guy. The guy yelled that he was going to sue.

Mike went to the office and went invisible and looked at the doctor's files and then went further into his background and found out that the guy had his license revoked in another state. Mike bought this to the attention of the hospital staff. The doc was fired and Mike told him, "Next time you had better know who you are dealing with when you try to take on someone." Chang died and Mike had his lawyer sue the doctor for Chang"s family for malpractice

and won. He gave all the money he got from the lawsuit to Chang's family. He took on his hobbies full-time and fully enjoyed it. Sometimes the Changs would plan something and they would swarm all over the place. Some of the kids washed his cars, others the boat, and some cleaned the living quarters. When he asked them, "Why did you do it?" They told him it was their way of paying him back for all he did for their family.

He took the boat out and was fishing and made the decision to quit. He was taking on some cases, but he decided to fully quit.

THE END

TRANSPARENT DETECTIVE---2

Arthur Allen

CHAPTER ONE

Mike Johnson sat in his recliner watching his favorite movie. His

dogs lay at his feet, two beautiful German Shepherds. One was named

George (after General Patton), the other was named Chesty (after a Marine general). He had just put his cup down when the heads of the dogs jerked up and they rose and went to the door. Mike jumped up, went to the window, and saw two men getting out of a car. They walked to the doorand he heard the buzzer go off.

He went to the panel that contained the button to activate and deactivate the alarm system; it also contained a speaker system that

allowed him to ask who was at the door.

"Who is it?" he asked.

"Mr. Johnson? We are from the FBI and we are here to ask you something."

He buzzed them in and said, "Come on up."

He went to the side table and took out his .45 caliber pistol and put it on the table next to his chair. The men came into the room and the dogs watched them intently. The men saw thje dogs and stopped.

Mike said, "Boys, heel, "and the dogs backed off. The men looked around and saw the pistol.

The taller of the two said, "I'm Joe Miller. This is Jake Simon."

They produced identification. Mike took them, looked them over and motioned for them to sit. As they did, the dogs watched them carefully. "Okay, gents, what's the problem?" he asked.

Miller said, "We are having trouble taking down a drug dealer and murderer. There is someone inside our organization that is

tipping off the dealers and we can't find them. We were hoping you could help us in that department."

"What makes you think I can help?" Mike asked.

"You are well-known in the FBI and other departments, although we don't know what makes you so different from us." Simon asked with a hint of sarcasm in his voice.

Miller looked at him and said, "You don't need to know."

Mike told them, "I'll think about it and get back to you."

They rose from the couch and Miller said, "We need to know soon."

Mike said, "I'll let the department know," and motioned them toward the door.

After they left he went to the south wall of his den and pressed a button under his desk. The wall slid back to expose a room filled with computer and radio equipment. He sat at the keyboard and contacted the boss man at the FBI and asked him about the men who had just left. He confirmed the fact and asked Mike if he would help. Mike typed in that he would.

He left the room and slid the panel back in place, then summoned Chang and told him to pack a couple of suitcases and ask his father to accompany him on this trip. Chang acknowledged with a bow and left to do as he was told.

Mike went to his den and packed his camera and tape recorder and a couple of pistols in a bag. He also took a small bottle of the liquid that made him invisible; he wouldn't need much, but just in case. After he finished he returned to his movie and a beer. A couple of hours later, the movie was over and he went to bed, but first he let the dogs out to do their thing and let them back in when they had finished. They followed him to his bedroom and lay on the floor as he went to bed.

In the morning he and Chang, the older of the two, left for the airport.

Chang was the man who helped Mike when he got to Hong Kong after escaping from the Chinese prison camp. They became not only employee and employer, but also long time friends. Chang was a martial arts master and a great asset to Mike.

They got to the airport and picked up their tickets at the counter as Chang #2 had called last night and made arrangements. Both men went to first class and were seated together. Chang immediately went to sleep, or so someone who didn't know him would think, so Mike took out a book and began to read. They ate when the time came to do so and talked for a while.

They landed and rented a car and went to a hotel that Mike had stayed in before and was remembered and treated well. They went to their suite and, as Chang took care of the contents of the bags, Mike made a couple of phone calls, one to the FBI office there in New York and one to the headman. He hung up before the call went through. He thought if they had a man who was an informant for the drug dealer, they would know he was here if he called in. He decided to go invisible and look around and listen and film all the things he saw and heard.

CHAPTER TWO

After dinner in their room, Mike told Chang his plans and asked him to

try to find out anything he could in the neighborhood of Chinatown. Chang was the consummate man's man; he had called ahead for a car and room in this hotel before going to the airport to board a plane,

Chang came out of his room in peasant clothing, his disguise for the mission.

"You look like a peasant and good job, old friend!" Mike exclaimed.

"That is my intent, sir," Chang replied and he slipped out of the door. He unpacked his camera and other equipment, headed for the shower and, turning on the hot water, stepped in and relaxed to the beat of the hot water on his scarred body. After drying off and changing into pajamas, he went to bed for a well deserved rest

He awoke and, after ordering breakfast and eating it, he again showered and then took his ring and filled the small compartment with fluid and then called the

FBI office and made an appointment with the headman.

Before leaving, he placed hairs on the closet and drawers in the room.

This would tell him if anyone was snooping in his room. He packed his equipment in an oversized briefcase, his camera, recorder, and books and

went down to the lobby and into the garage for his car. He went to the FBI and his appointment with the director of the New York office.

When he went into the office, he informed the woman that he had an appointment. she checked and said, "Oh, yes. This way please."

He followed her into a plush office." Mr. Yates, this is Mike Johnson," and she left.

The guy stood and extended his hand, "Bob Yates."

Mike said, "Hi, Bob.

What is it you wanted?"

Bob sat and began, "I've heard about you and I'm not a believer in this, but my people persist." He stood and went to the window. When he did, Mike turned his ring and vanished. When Bob turned, he gaped at the chair Mike was in and gasped, "What the hell...Where," and his pen set rose off the desk and moved to the edge of the desk. Bob jumped back andMike laughed.

"Ha! Ha! Bob it's me," and he appeared next to the man.

Bob sat at his desk and told him that he had a spy in his office and couldn't find him. Mike told him he would find the person, but Bob was not to say anything about him being here.

He left the office, went to the first floor and into the men's room where he switched over. He left the briefcase: it was empty. He had the camera and recorder in his pockets and he started into the drug team task force room.

Chapter Three

He went into the room and stood and listened to the men talking, then he wandered around the room. He watched the man in the corner on the computer and watched as the man worked the keys. A movement to his right caught his attention and he watched as a woman went to the small room that was off to the left. He followed and watched as she picked up the phone and punched in some numbers, which he memorized. His recorder came out and was near her as she spoke,"It's me. I need to see you, I have some info. Four? Okay, I'll be there." She hung up and looked at the clock.

She picked up her purse and left. He followed and as she got into her car, he opened the door on the passenger side and got in. She gasped and said, "What the hell?" As the door closed, she started her car and took off. She turned left and went out of the city and after an hour turned into a driveway.

The guy at the gate said, "Hi, babe, he's expecting you," and directed her in.

When she got out he waited, then he got out and followed her into the house, which was a mansion. He followed her into a den.

The guy was seated behind a massive des., He was a man of Italian descent and was about six feet tall. There were two men standing behind him.

Mike started the camera and panned the room. He went to each man and
then to the boss man.

"Well, what is all the excitement about?" as he motioned her to a chair.

She sat in the chair crossing her legs and the two guys standing ogled her.

She said, "They are planning a raid on your warehouse in Jersey at nine, two nights from tonight. I thought you would like me to come out in person, Carlo."

He grinned, rose, and went to her, extending his hand and as she stood up, he handed her an envelope, "Thanks, Marie, there is more where that came from," and he led her out of the room and up the stairs. Mike followed. They went to his bedroom where they got naked and made love. Mike didn't film that part.

He went back to the den and, while the other men were gone, Mike went through the desk filming all the stuff he thought the FBI could use. He then went out the front door and then out to the street and back to the hotel.

Chang was there when he got there, "What did you find my friend?" he asked Chang.

Chang began, "The triads will begin to try to take over the drug trade in a week and they will start with Tony Marselli's place. They plan to take his warehouse in jersey in a week and they will be getting more men from China in three days." They had ordered a meal then when the mess was cleared, they cleaned up and went to sleep.

In the morning Mike was at the FBI office giving the tapes to the boss man who had the woman arrested and notified NIS of the Chinese deal.

They stayed to see what they could do in Chinatown. Mike went invisible and, using the superstitions of the people, went into the offices of the Tongs and enjoyed moving things around, causing the people *to think the place was haunted, and they ran off.*

After doing so, Mike scooped up all the papers and anything else he thought the FBI could use. When he took the stuff into the office, Bob went

Into a very happy state. "Oh man, this stuff will shut them down and deport most of them. I'll get this stuff over to INS ASAP," he happily exclaimed. "Mike, I don't know what to say, sorry I doubted you. Oh, the local P.D.can use a little help."

"I'll look into it," Mike said.

CHAPTER FOUR

Bob had called the chief of police in New York and Mike went to see him.

"We don't need any help from a weirdo," he snarled and turned his back.. When he did, Mike went invisible and when the man turned again, he smiled, "Good. The weirdo is gone." At that moment, the phone rose off its cradle and flew across his desk. "What the hell?" and he reached for it,

put it on the cradle. As he started to sit, the chair moved and he fell to the floor. "What the hell is going on here?" he yelled and got up and pulled the chair to him. A ghostly laugh bounded off the walls of his office. He looked around and Mike appeared to him. "Well, Chief, still think I'm a weirdo?"

The chief scowled, "You son of a bitch, I should lock you up."

Mike smiled and said, "On what charges?" and left the office and returned to the hotel where

Chang told him that the triads were going to hit the warehouse that night. Mike *phoned the cops and told them. He sat for a while,*

thinking, and called Chang, "I would like you to tape some things in Chinese." He knew that the Chinese people were superstitious and planned to act on that.

Mike took the tape and, along with Chang, went to the triad headquarters and it turned out to be the home of the leader. Chang had gotten himself into the gang and earned their trust and Mike went in as his invisible self and

waited for the men to gather in a large room. When they did and began talking, he began playing the tape. The room got deathly quiet and eyes wide as the men heard the cries and statements. The older men screamed and ran from yelling that their ancestors were there and not happy with them.

They went to their chapel to pray and then packed to leave the country. The younger ones didn't; they laughed at the older ones. Mike laughed to himself knowing that they would be in jail before the night was over. He and Chang left the place and returned to the hotel and waited. As they

ate their dinner, a call came in from the FBI stating that the triad was in custody, a few were shot and killed in a gun fight. They thankedMike for the job. They suggested he go to Washington, D.C. and the FBI offices there.

CHAPTER FIVE

They landed at the airport in Washington and were met by an agent who drove them to the FBI headquarters. They were led to the director's office and there received a plaque for the work. Mike asked that this not get into the paper, knowing full well that they wouldn't or couldn't
do it.

Mike decided to stay over a couple of days. He wanted to see the Vietnam memorial and they went to a hotel and cleaned up then had dinner. Chang had found that the leader of the triad had a home in Washington

As a matter of fact, they were in Washington because Chang was doing something for the triad and was due to go to the leader's home.

After dinner they left for the leader's home. On the way, Mike went into his invisible form and the tape recorder was in his pocket. Chang explained, "Remember, sir, these people are superstitious and the things on the tape should do what we want," which was to drive him out of the *house where he had been held up for a while. The FBI also wanted him.*

Chang went in the front door and Mike was right behind him. He went into the den and there was the old man. His name was Mau. He was in his late eighties and frail. He was on the phone and just hung it up and was looking into the fire in the fireplace. Mike switched on the recorder and the old man's eyes opened wide. When Mike took a vase and moved it from a table to the mantle, the old man screamed"EEEEiiiiiiiiiiiiiiiiiiiiiiii" and the door flew open and his bodyguards and Chang came running in with pistols drawn.

The old man's face was white and he was shaking. He babbled about ghosts and the men tried to comfort him. When the vase sailed from the fireplace to smash aginst the wall, the other men stared wide-eyed and began to quickly move the old man out of the den. The spooky

sounds continued and as they looked back they saw a letter opener coming at them. One stopped and tried to stop it, but Mike took it and threw it. It stuck in the wall next to the man. They were all out the front door, right into the hands of the FBI who had been called by Mike before he went there.

Mike returned to the den and the desk. He went through it and then went to the computer. He found a password in a drawer and brought up all the stuff on the triad: personnel, imports, drugs, and prostitution.

Mike turned his ring, went visible, put all the information on a pouch, and twisted the ring, disappearing, just as a man came into the room. Mike moved away from the computer and picked up his video camera. As the man moved to the computer, he filmed the whole thing.

It turned out this guy was the old man's lawyer and he was outraged that he could find nothing on the computer. One of the old Chinese men came in, "What the hell?" he scowled.

"Hey, I was..." the lawyer shouted as he raised his hands and moved away from the desk. The Chinese man pulled a gun and as he held it on the lawyer, he moved to the computer and, looking at it, he scowled,

"Why, you cheating son of a pig," and he shot the man.

The sound of the gun going off echoed around the room. Mike winced at the sound. The lawyer was thrown back aginst the wall by the force of the shot and, as the Chinese man moved toward him, a cop entered the room, "Freeze! Police! Don't move, drop the weapon." The Chinaman made a foolish move: he turned toward the cop, his pistol coming up. The cop put three shots into him and his shot went over the cop's head and fell to the floor, dead.

Mike went out the door and as he went to his car he became visible. When the head of the FBI in New York came to him, he handed over all

the information he had.

"Thanks, Mike. We couldn't have done it with out you. Come to my office in the morning and I'll have your check for you."

Mike thanked him and got into his car. He went to the police station.

He was going to play a little with the chief. He went to the rest room, became invisible, and then went to the chief's *office. He entered when another officer went in and waited. When the officer left, Mike moved the pen the chief used, it was a fountain pen the type that used a lever to fill it.*

The chief said, "What the hell?" The pen went up and turned toward him, the lever went up and a stream of ink shot at the chief's chest.

Mike said, "Weird scams, huh Chief? Well, this isn't weird." He dropped the pen and left. The chief yelled, "Stop him! Stop him!" Everyone looked around to see what he was looking at. Mike went into the rest room and changed back and left.

CHAPTER SIX

He went back to the hotel and instructed Chang to pack up. They were going back home when Chang put his finger to silence him. Mike went invisible as the door was kicked in and three armed men rushed.

Chang used a high martial art's spin kick, catching the leader in the head, dropping him. Mike hit the second in the throat, breaking his windpipe. The third just stood there gawking. He was looking at the place where the second man was and seeing nothing, he began to turn when he was grabbed from behind and pulled back into the room.

He was pulled to a chair and pushed into it. Chang asked him, "Who sent you?"

When he didn't answer, Mike, still invisible, picked up one of the pistols that had been dropped and came toward the man, whose eyes grew wide and he began to squirm and mumble. He was beginning to cry and he began to babble out the information they wanted. Chang called the police, and when they came, they explained what went on. Then they left.

They were assigned another room until they left. The next day they went after the man who had sent the thugs after them. He was the grandson of the old man who was arrested two nights before. They came upon him in a house on the edge of one of the boroughs and went in. Mike was in his invisible state. Chang was known to them and they asked where Mike was, the young one was grabbed from behind in a choke hold.

Mike told the men, "If you move to stop me, I'll break his neck." They backed away and as they looked around, the police arrived. They had been called beforeMike and Chang went in.

They were all cuffed and taken away. Mike and Chang returned to the hotel and a call was waiting. They could go home, but would have to return when the trial began. They were on the airplane for an hour when two men stood and yelled that this was a hijack and one ran to the cockpit.

Mike quickly got up while they weren't looking and went to thje restroom. He came out and went to the hijacker in the *cabin and applied pressure to the pressure point in his neck. The man fell. Chang quickly went to him tied him up and waited.*

A call came from the cockpit. It was repeated and when no answer came, he came out of the cockpit. Mike grabbed him and Chang grabbed his gun and they took him out. He was also tied up and the pilot called ahead to have them jailed and Mike went into the restroom to change back.

They landed in San Diego and his driver was waiting. He and Chang put the luggage in the trunk and they started for home. Mike was given a pile of messages and was going through them. He saw one from his brother and immediately called him. His mom and dad had died and they went in their sleep. He would make arrangements, but Mike wouldn't be there. He had never gotten along with his folks. They were aginst him joining the Marines and when he was captured they disowned him for making them sad. The people who were aginst the war had harassed them.

They were in the airport and a man came in and tried to steal his bag. Mike tripped him and, as the man tried to get up, he kicked his hands out from under him and put his foot in the middle of thje guy's back to hold him until the police got there. Chang went and got the car and they went

home. When they got there, Mike said, "Chang, something is wrong." They stopped the car and slowly advanced toward the building. They went in the side door and there was one of the dogs, dead. It had been shot. Mike

grabbed Chang and went invisible. He stepped into the gym. The other dog was there; it, too, had been shot. This pissed Mike off and he slowly went up the stairs to the living room. There was one of his people on the floor. He, too, had been shot.

Mike went through the place and found two more of his people. Both had been loyal and trustworthy friends and both were Chang's sons. Chang stayed and was

kneeling by the body of his youngest. Mike called the police and then tried to comfort his old friend. He went into the bathroom to get a damp cloth and there he *saw some writing on his mirror: wait for a phone call.*

The police came and Mike told them that he and Chang had just gotten home from the East Coast. He told them all he knew and they did all their investigating. Mike would do his own later.

CHAPTER SEVEN

The writing on the mirror was in Chinese and Mike could read a little.

He told Chang about the message and after the bodies were moved, they waited for the phone to ring. A few hours it did and Chang was told to go to an old abandoned warehouse in the waterfront district. Mike took his video camera and went along. As they neared the docks, he went invisible and told Chang he would be near.

When they stopped at the location they got out of the car using the same doorway so they wouldn't see both or know both were there.

Two men approached and they spoke to Chang, "You are the one who is responsible for our grandfather's death. He died in jail and you will pay."

One of them grabbed for him and they paid for it. Chang used a form of Karate to disable them and Mike called the police. Two more came out of the darkness and Mike, using martial arts, took them out. Both had looks of surprise as they looked around to see what or who had hit them.

Three more came out of the darkness; they had guns and were pointing them at Chang. Mike kicked the one nearest him and as the man looked at his partner, Chang did a high spin kick hitting the man at the point of his jaw, breaking it and driving it into his brain, killing him. At this time the police arrived and Mike came visible. He explained the presence of the men and the circumstances of the fight. The men were arrested and taken away.

Mike and Chang returned home and cleaned up. Mike went to bed and Chang went to the morgue to see his sons and make arrangements for their funeral. Mike told him he would take care of the expenses. He took the dogs and went to bed. Nine hours later, Chang was waking him to a breakfast of hot cakes, eggs, sausage, hash browns, and coffee. He showered, dressed, and went to the dining room. Chang served him and asked, "Sir, if it is okay with you, I would like to bring some more of my family here."

Mike told him, "Okay, old friend, and I'll pay for it, give me the phone."

Mike called an old friend at Immigration and asked if he could help in bringing some people in the country and explained to him who it was.

The man in INS said, "I'll see what I can do."

He put the phone down and when it rang he answered it. It was the police. They were going to prosecute the men who attacked them in the park and the rest in New York were in jail and it was certain they would be prosecuted.

Mike went through the building to see what damage the men had did and found it wasn't much. He worked out in the gym for a couple of hours and went upstairs for lunch and a shower, then went out to the boat to check it out and get it ready to go fishing. He was mopping the deck when a car pulled up. It was Mike's old friend from the police department. Since it was close to dinnertime, Mike asked him to stay and Lieutenant Chuck Combs agreed.

He had come to tell Mike that the men who attacked them were in prison and *wouldn't see daylight for a long time. They were charged with murder, the murder of Chang's sons. They ate and chatted and made a date to go fishing, and Chuck left.*

It was seven months later that Chang's relatives arrived and they were so happy they wanted to work for Mike, so he set them up in a house and put the boys to work. Chang taught them how to maneuver the boat and how to work on it and the cars. His oldest daughter became his cook.and housekeeper, but the place was so large that the others helped her to keep house. Mike provided for them and sponsored them in this country.

The boys went to school and liked it and were good in school. The date for Mike and Chuck's fishing date arrived and Chuck bought the beer and Mike the food. They left at dawn and were at the place they wanted to be at about eight and spent the day there fishing.

They docked at about five in the afternoon and the boys took the fish to clean as Mike and Chuck went to thje Gym to watch a football game in the bar. Mike said, "Hey, buddy, why don't we make this a regular thing on weekends that unless we're busy, we get together on weekends to fish, watch football, or lift weights or just spend the weekends together." Chuck agreed the phone rang and it was for Chuck. After he hung up he said, "That was the FBI, they put the triads in prison and broke its back and they want to give you an award."

Mike told him, "Chuck, I don't want an award."

After Chuck left, Mike went to his den and brought his records up to date.

He closed out the file on the triads and was just closing the file cabinet when Chang's grandson came into the den with his lunch. "Thank you,

Wan-lei," he said and the boy bowed and left. Mike called Chang via the intercom and when he got there he told him to ask his boy not to bow. It made him uncomfortable in that he wasn't used to it, although he knew it was a sign of respect.

"Mike, I told them, but they are so grateful for the fact that you are responsible for them being here that they want to do it."

Mike said, "Okay, I don't want to interfere with their beliefs."

After Chang left,

Mike went to his room and put on his swimsuit. He was going to swim in the ocean near the dock. He was in the water and after swimming for a while he heard some crying for help and noticed a boy struggling and he went down. Mike dove down and pulled the boy up and took him to the dock.

Chang's kids were working on the boat and dock. When he pulled the boy out of the water, he yelled, "Call 911!" and he started CPR and was bringing the boy around when the paramedics arrived. They took the boy to the hospital for a check up. Mike asked them, "Keep me informed." He hadn't mentioned the bruises he had seen on the boy. He went to the phone and called Chuck.

"What's up, Mike?" Chuck asked.

He told Chuck about the boy and asked him to look into the fact that the boy might have been abused.

Later that dayMike got a call from Chuck, " Sorry, man. The kid died, but not *from the water it was from the beating from his dad. We picked him up an hour ago."*

Mike thanked him and slammed down the phone.

Chang came into the room and Mike told him of the boy dying and the circumstances of it. He sat with his head in his hands and remembered that it was times like this that the hobby room used to calm him. He tried it. He went down to the hobby room and rummaged through the models until he found one he would build and started in on it. Chang came into the room and informed him that it was past midnight Mike exclaimed, "Hot damn! I got all wound up in this model that I hadn't looked at the clock."

He put it away and went up to bed.

In the morning he had a breakfast of waffles, sausage, toast, juice, and coffee, then he went down to the hobby room to finish the model. He had just finished painting it when the phone rang.

It was Chuck, "Hey, Mike, I have a person here who wants you to find someone for her."

Mike told him, "Sorry, man. I'm retiring as of today.I'll see you on the weekend," and hung up.

The end

Arthur Allen

About the Author

The author is a Vietnam veteran who spent two tours in country, he also spent twenty years in the MARINE corps, some of the survival tricks he has used.

www.ingramcontent.com/pod-product-compliance
Lightning Source LLC
Chambersburg PA
CBHW030308290526
45785CB00001B/260